KT-453-534

# Sister Madeleine osa

## Solitary Refinement

SCM PRESS LTD

334  01496  4

*First published 1972*
*by SCM Press Ltd*
*56 Bloomsbury Street London*

© *SCM Press Ltd 1972*

*Printed in Great Britain by*
*Richard Clay (The Chaucer Press) Ltd*
*Bungay, Suffolk*

*To my dear mother,*
*with love*

# Contents

# 1    The Question Why

'It's like this, Sister,' said the driver of the minicab. 'Suppose I had only five shillings and was very, very hungry, but went on starving rather than spend my money, I reckon that would be sin. Original sin, if you like – hoarding, not living for fear of dying. Well, aren't you doing the same? Why aren't you spending your life and vitality in marriage and in the world at large? Why ever did a nice girl like you become a nun?'

Always the question 'Why?' From friends and acquaintances, from patients and pupils, from Christians and non-Christians. And usually the question is loaded, as it is above, presuming the answer to be in negative terms of withdrawal and fear – fear of love, sex, pleasure, competition; a refusal to live for fear of spiritual death.

It is easy enough to understand the question and the assumptions behind it. Everyone wants to fulfil themselves in love, in responsibility, in freedom. But it is not immediately obvious, to say the least, that this could happen in a form of existence in which sex is something you are, not something you do; where possessions are used, not owned; where freedom of choice is more than ordinarily limited.

On the whole, at least in the West, religious life is at present regarded as one of the least attractive forms of opting out of society. Unbelievers, who in any case feel that religion is an illusion, 'the opium of the people', see the religious life as a logical conclusion to a death-wish, the consequence of the trickery exercised by the God-myth. For middle-of-the-road people, religious are 'outsiders' who bewilderingly reject a normal way of life. For believers, they are often those who pervert the gospel, the good news that 'the glory of God is man fully alive', in a vain attempt to be justified by asceticism rather than by faith. In fewer and fewer countries are religious immediately acceptable, even to Christians. It is no longer clear why their work in education, social welfare, art, literature and so on should go hand in hand with a special life-form: with a celibacy which is lived out sometimes in solitude but more often in community, and an asceticism which at least forbids private possession of goods and demands obedience to a life-directing rule.

The unusually articulate cab-driver expressed the usual objection very well. He spoke of 'hoarding', and indeed, for many, monks and nuns are persons who understand religion to pose a false option: *either* this world *or* the next, *either* human love *or* divine love, *either* mediocrity *or* integrity of the spirit. It seems to these people as though religious believe that the only way in which they can keep intact life's gifts of love and freedom without allowing them to stain the soul or to result in passionate attachment to persons and things is to renounce the possibility of marriage and possessions.

Leaving on one side the question whether such a picture of religious life could ever be acceptable to Christians (could it be reconciled with the fundamental emphasis of the Bible on creativity?), we ought to note that the idea that religious life is a flight from the pain and passion of secularity is in some measure due to the kind of responses that religious themselves make to the question 'Why?' The outsider often finds these responses obscure and inadequate. But that is not necessarily a proof that the choice of the religious life is either so other-worldly or so irrational that it demands secrecy and silence. First of all, there is the quite common difficulty of giving verbal form to experiences – like falling in love – which seem to be done both by us and to us, which affect our being as a whole and fuse value, thought and feeling into one free yet inevitable direction. 'Monks,' wrote Thomas Merton, 'do not expect to be understood by men because they do not fully understand themselves. They are too much part of the mystery to be able to formulate an apologetic for their own lives.'[1] The 'mystery' is not the comparative strangeness of voluntary celibacy or communal possessions or constant prayer. These are no more than possible conditions and expressions of living the mystery that is man's capacity for self-transcending love and for relationship with God. Only if it is set within the context of such a relationship can religious life and its apparent negations be seen, not as a vocation for renouncement but as renouncement for a vocation.

For religious, 'vocation' is a very important concept indeed and a very complex one – more complex, perhaps, than appears at first sight. It has a tone of finality about it. It tends to silence objections rather like a 'disabled driver' notice. If you ask your best friend why he has parked himself in a monastery for the rest of his life, what can you say if he replies that it is not his own choice but a divine election? There is perhaps a kind of naïveté here, not only in the actual words but in the understanding which they express. What is meant when people talk about vocation is not always what might seem to be meant.

Take some examples from real life. 'I experienced a direct call to the life.' 'God has designed from all eternity that some of us should be nuns and has therefore given us the qualities of mind and heart to do so.' 'I fought for a long time against the conviction that this was God's will for me, but it was this conviction which brought me and kept me here.' 'I could not refuse what God was ever more clearly asking.' 'I was told I had a vocation.' 'My decision was really the Lord's, I had only to recognize it.' These quotations might suggest that the choice of religious life, unlike, say, that of marriage, was imposed upon a person from outside. It might seem that there was no weighing up of alternatives in terms of what attracted the person and what his or her aptitudes happened to be. But this is not what the remarks mean. When they talk about vocation, religious first of all seek to affirm that they have not made a purely arbitrary decision. If one were to enter a profession such as nursing or teaching with little idealism, simply because the work was secure and useful, possibly satisfying and moderately well-paid, this would not be regarded as a disqualification. But the religious life has to be chosen primarily with reference to God's plan of love for the world and his desire for each individual's growth in Christ-like wholeness. The choice is made in a deep spirit of faith that tries to discern the best way for a given individual to realize the wholeness in love which is God's will for us all. Furthermore, religious seek to stress in their talk of 'vocation' that they have not just chosen an impersonal way of life. Just as one does not really

11

choose marriage, but responds to a person with whom one desires to share all of one's life, so one does not choose the vowed religious state for itself, but seeks to live it as an evoked response to a personal God.

How is a 'call' made known? Sometimes the explanations of religious suggest that they experience a special revelation in a mystical manner. But this is not always what they mean to convey. These people speak from the assumption, a biblical one, that life is a kind of dialogue with God, whose words come to us in and through the persons, events, situations of everyday living. By a variety of ways, odd or ordinary, a person can be led to an overwhelming desire to embrace monastic life. If they do so, it is because this desire is interpreted by them as an invitation, as a call from God. 'Interpret' is perhaps the key word. Even religious themselves do not always understand that to label various elements of one's experience a 'vocation' is not so much to state a fact as to interpret facts in the light of certain assumptions – assumptions about God's providence and how this providence works within human freedom. If these assumptions are not shared by others, then the inferences drawn from the language may differ considerably from the meaning intended.

One could equally well answer the question 'Why?' in personal, subjective terms. One could say: 'I have chosen, I have been attracted, I have thought this good for me. I have decided that, taking everything into account, this is the best way for me to realize what life is all about.' But we shall learn a great deal from considering the persistence of such language as 'I have been called, chosen, graced, elected by God.' These expressions throw into relief the role of God in the affair. They are obviously natural to people steeped in the scriptures. The Bible notoriously omits secondary causes in order to make dramatically apparent the activity of God, the First Cause. (The trouble is that the relationship between the two might be badly misunderstood.) It is written that Abraham was *called* by God to leave his country and his father's house, that Moses was *commanded* to lead his people out of Egypt and slavery, that the prophets were *appointed* by the Lord and could not do other than prophesy. Indeed the whole people of Israel had the experience of being a *chosen* nation, elected by their God as a special instrument of his plan for the world. Similarly in the New Testament the apostles were *summoned* by Christ: 'Come, follow me.' St John has Christ tell them: 'You have not chosen me, but I have chosen you.'

Now such language is for the most part *interpretative* rather than purely descriptive. Moses' role in the liberation of the Israelites could, without contradiction, have been described exclusively in terms of that blend of sensitivity, responsibility and political skill which fits a man to become a great natural leader. Yet the Bible attributes all – the initiative, the sensitivity, the responsibility, to God, in the belief that history and human affairs are the field of God's presence and power. They are perceived as such by those who 'have eyes to see' – the prophets whose spiritual gift is precisely that of interpreting events and natural causes with reference to God's plan.

When we religious try to explain ourselves to people who do not share our assumptions, we ought to remember the problems and the complexities of biblical talk about vocation; indeed, we ought to consider whether it is the best language to use. Yet we cannot forget its wealth of insight. How much poorer we should be if the Bible gave us merely phenomenal, observable, one-dimensional history! It is precisely because the Bible does disclose to us the divine dimension, the presence of the transcendent Other in people's situations, addressing them with the voice of those situations, needs and possibilities, that it is of value to us. Similarly, we should all be poorer in religious awareness if there were not people, among them monks and nuns, who speak to us of discovering themselves only in terms of being discovered, of finding their way in life only in terms of being found, of choosing in terms of being chosen by God. 'It is not we who seek the way,' wrote Dag Hammarskjöld, 'but the way which seeks us. That is why you are faithful to it.'[2]

Something quite central to faith is behind the rather naïve expression 'I have a vocation'. It is that 'all is grace, is gift', both the fullness of life to which we are called and the ability to respond in different ways to the call. The expression also conveys something quite central to love, for discernment of the beloved's intentions is all-important for the realization of the union that love seeks. So a religious may find it a little difficult to say to his questioners: 'I am attracted to this life; I find it good and beautiful; I feel it offers me possibilities for fulfilling myself.' For he already knows that it was not the attraction itself that mattered, but the fact that it mediated the will of God for his particular life. The reason why, in convents and monasteries, a person is not permitted for several years to engage himself definitively in the form of life that he or she desires is that this desire has first to be tested in the fire of discernment, in prayer, reflection, counsel, growing self-knowledge and an assessment of the overall effects of the life upon his human and Christian growth. As Kierkegaard put it: 'It is only the truth which edifies which is the truth for me.'

There are other reasons, mostly unadmitted, for speaking as if it were God alone and not one's heart and human freedom and self-concern that brought one to religious life. They are to do with a fear of things that go bump in the night – of our subconscious! Motivations in general, and religious motivations in particular, are rarely simple and clear; they are more often complex and tangled. We tend to expose, even to ourselves, only those motives that are rational or socially acceptable. The fear that these seemingly substantial reasons should be reduced to 'nothing but' rationalizations prevents us from looking into the self's subrational underworld or allowing others to do so. It might appear, for example, that the word 'love' is nothing but a rationalization if we admit that because of childhood deprivation we are hoping to gain security and protection from marriage or religious life. But in fact, simply because there are inadequate, nonrational factors that strongly influence our choices, it does not follow that all our acceptable, reasonable self-explanations are 'nothing but' the subtle masks of a devious subconscious. Almost all our upright and honourable choices have a shadowy background in which lurk the traces of infantilism and emotional distortion. It is possible that many a doctor or social worker has undertaken his profession *both* through a positive interest in it, a genuine desire to alleviate distress, *and* an unacknowledged need to be needed or to appease some form of sub-rational guilt. The important thing is to become aware of the existence in ourselves of these sub-rational dynamisms and of the nature and extent of their influence.

Religious are such an easy prey for superficial psychologizing. This may be one reason why they seem to prefer the extreme objectivity of explanations such as 'I have been called by God', for it shifts the whole initiative of their choice from the confused sphere of subjectivity, where it is difficult to know whether conscious, adequate motives disguise or simply co-exist with unconscious compulsions, fears and drives. In fact, of course, there may be elements such as the desire for spiritual or emotional security, fear of marriage, a compulsive need for order and discipline, childish other-worldliness, among their motives. The individual must be helped to become aware of these and to assess whether they are primary or secondary determinations. For they may be secondary and in no way disprove the existence or authenticity of a desire to spend oneself for others in love and service, or a deep-seated conviction that one's human, spiritual growth could be best served within a religious community.

Here again can be seen the necessity and very great importance of a long and delicately handled period of probation before commitment by vows within the religious state. Indeed, at the present time the decision to accept a person even as a candidate for the novitiate is becoming ever more serious and circumspect. For inevitably entrance to religious life is sought not only by persons with predominantly inadequate motivations but often by those suffering from very deep and possibly disguised personality disorders – religious mania, arrested development, deformed psycho-sexuality, neurotic timidity and so on. The cloister represents a 'heaven-haven' for them all, to use Gerard Manley Hopkins' poetic, if somewhat misleading phrase. Just as unacceptable are those whose 'vocation' is nothing but a web of fantasies spun by the rubbishy romanticism of various films or novels. Refusing all these people admission to the life is not snobbish perfectionism. Nobody wants to, and nobody could, claim that religious are the *crème de la crème* of psychological fitness! It is simply a question of recognizing that such persons are not in fact choosing religious life, but a projection of their imagination or a refuge from reality. Moreover, in most of these cases, the component elements of the life – celibacy, obedience, community, prayer – could only be lived in a manner that would distort their purpose and aggravate the subject's condition. For example, celibacy might be lived as a flight from sexuality, obedience as irresponsible passivity, community as sheltering collectivism and prayer as reverie and escapist fantasy. It simply is not the *raison d'être* of religious communities (in themselves, as distinct from in their work) to be therapeutic societies for the maladjusted and neurotic. It is reasonable to demand, therefore, that before acceptance a candidate be seen to possess enough spiritual and affective maturity, as well as adequate intellectual and physical capacities, for there to be at least a real possibility of a vocation to live according to the ideal and aims of a particular community. To help assess psychological fitness, many communities now require candidates to be screened by a psychologist or trained counsellor. His role is simply to indicate certain psychological factors that may be relevant. These indications should be neither under- nor over-estimated.

For, as Karl Stern points out in *The Third Revolution*,[3] man does not end where psychology ends. The psychologist's assistance in the process of discernment is limited. He may be able to indicate that a person is neither so immature nor so neurotic that their choice of religious life is invalid from the outset. But a community should not be looking primarily for maturity in a candidate (still less for a certain personality type). It should be looking for inspiration, faith and love – qualities paradoxically nearer to madness than to sweet reason and common sense. It is not a common-sense decision to 'become a eunuch for the sake of the kingdom of heaven', to take the desert route of sexual solitude in the common human journey towards the fullness of love. Reason knows quite well that less barren ways lead to the same objective. Or rather, only when reason is mature enough to know this can a free choice of an alternative be made. So, neat and tidy models of balance, of ordered behaviour and self-possession, who want nothing else than to do a good deed a day for the rest of their lives, are just as much to be suspected of mistaking the nature of the enterprise as the various kinds of refugees from reality.

It is probably true to say that many excellent persons who feel called to dedicate themselves to some form of service in society request admission to a religious order for purely pragmatic reasons. The community offers them affective support and/or an

16

organization that makes for greater opportunities and efficiency in the service. Thus many men who wish to become priests in the Roman Catholic church prefer to do so as members of a religious community because that gives them companionship to offset the loneliness of celibacy as well as possibilities for a specialized ministry and a geographically wide-ranging one. Here there is not a positive desire for the religious form of life, nor the positive need to deepen the life of the spirit from within the specific human condition created by the vows of celibacy, poverty and obedience. One could say that these men have become religious simply because, until now, there have been so few satisfying alternative forms of life.

This may be the case, too, for many brothers in teaching and nursing orders. A teaching brother wrote recently to the *National Catholic Reporter* suggesting that the vows taken by members of his order were such an obstacle that the order's work in education was threatened with gradual extinction. The *raison d'être* of the order, he said, was the apostolic ministry in Christian schools, and the vows were in no way necessary for this to be done in a wholly dedicated way. He is, of course, right up to a point, but the religious life cannot be identified completely with any particular apostolate. There should be many different kinds of community, co-operative, association or commune in the church, so that vows should not have to be taken as part of a package deal. Only those whose spiritual needs require the way of celibate love for God and man for their fulfilment should choose the specifically religious or monastic way.

A person who enters religious life may wait anything from three to nine years before making a final commitment by vow. The first period is often called the postulancy – it is more a time of assessment than of preparation. The aim is to try to discern the plan of God in the life of the person drawn towards religious life in a particular community. So the postulant is given the possibility of experiencing realistically the community's spirit, work and life-style, to know and be known by the other members. The postulant may reside, work or study either within or outside the community. But he or she needs to have sufficient periods of time in the monastery or convent and enough guidance and in-

17

struction to make a truly prudent first assessment of suitability for the life.

Then comes the novitiate – a time of preparation for self-commitment to God within a particular religious community. It may last for one or two years, and aims to help the novice to know and respond to the demands of the vocation, to internalize and integrate its many aspects. Of primary importance in a novitiate is development in the art of prayer and human relationships. Ample opportunity is usually given for the study of scripture, theology, religious life, the history and spirit of the novice's community. It is to some extent a 'desert' experience, characterized by a certain withdrawal from intense exterior activity in order to pray, study and reflect. However, opportunities are, or should be, given for the novice to engage in whatever works are integral to the community's life, so that a gradual unity between contemplation and action is achieved.

Usually novices are the special responsibility of one member of the community, a director of novices. Moreover, in the past, they have been somewhat segregated from the professed members. This, however, is recognized today as being rather absurd and harmful. It is the total experience of life in and with the community that is educative for the novice. Happily it is also recognized that if initiation implies a sharing of knowledge, insight and wisdom with beginners, these latter are not exclusively receivers. They have much to contribute and must be allowed to join creatively with the rest of the community in shaping its life and modifying its structures and attitudes.

At the end of the novitiate a decision is made, both by the novice and the community, as to the rightness or not of a first commitment. This is a promise or vow establishing a bond and mutual responsibility between the community and the new member, who pledges himself to love and serve God with that particular community according to its ideals and aims. It is a commitment that cannot be made validly unless the novice at the time feels that religious life in this community is his or her place to be, to grow in all the dimensions of love a whole life long. But it is a pledge that the community will not allow most novices to make in the form of a permanently binding vow. The first commitment, therefore, is usually a temporary one, for it is felt that

18

a person may still not know himself or be mature enough after the novitiate to be vowed to God for ever within religious life. It can be anything from four to seven years after this first promise or vow before a permanent commitment is made.

Should there be a permanent commitment at all? That depends upon your view of love and its ways. For when all is said and done, that battered but still splendid and irreplaceable word 'love' is the only adequate answer to the question 'Why?'

## NOTES

1. Thomas Merton, *Silence in Heaven*, Studio Publications, New York 1956, p. 22.
2. Dag Hammarskjöld, *Markings*, Faber 1966, p. 107.
3. Michael Joseph 1955.

# 2 Objections

Something of the glory has departed from religious life – at least in the eyes of its beholders. So, too, have many of its members. Literally thousands of Roman Catholic religious have left their communities in the past six or seven years, since about the end of Vatican II. Ironically, during this time life in convents and monasteries has become immeasurably more pleasant, more exciting and on many levels more humanly satisfying than it had been for many years, in response to the council's call for religious life to be brought into touch with the contemporary world. This has meant that while basic values such as asceticism, silence, community, poverty, obedience, prayer have been retained, they have been reinterpreted in the light of modern psychology and sociology. This has done away with much of the cultural oddness and backwardness that used to characterize the religious life almost everywhere.

A combination of esteem for tradition and a degree of separation from surrounding society had caused a great cultural gap between religious communities and the world which was often perversely glorified as the sign of spiritual superiority. We can see a parallel instance of this in the way that, for example, hippie communes combine a distinctive style of life in dress and behaviour with a belief that the values which they embrace are superior to those of the social *status quo*. But whereas the modern drop-out tries to express creative freedom from traditions, spontaneity, imagination and originality in his counter-culture, the monastic society expressed merely a mummified past, a well-preserved antiquity, not only in its dress but also in its patterns of thought, of communication, of authority, of recreation and so on. However, the windows and doors have been opened, and in have blown healthy winds of cultural change.

Thus the number of hours devoted to work and prayer were reduced if they were found to be excessive, and in leisure time imposed communal forms of recreation began to disappear. It became more acceptable, at least for members of active orders, to go to a theatre or cinema, to eat out and take holidays with their families.

Previously, guests were never allowed further in a religious house than the parlour, the garden and the back benches of the chapel. Now they are often invited into the common room and the refectory, which no longer resembles a feudal lord's dining hall with long wooden tables where the seating was arranged in hierarchical order.

More important, the kind of effective democracy and participation in all levels of decision-making that is now demanded by students, workers, local governments, etc., has come into existence in many communities with startling rapidity. Methods and structures of dialogue which guaranteed a share of responsibility or at least consultation began to replace the old autocratic approach with its paternalistic reliance on good will and justice from 'superiors' towards subjects.

Liturgy – the eucharist and daily office – began to manifest somewhat timidly and awkwardly a degree of spontaneity and variety. French Jesuits strummed the guitar and African Carmelites danced like black shadows to the beating of their drums after the consecration at Mass.

Sisters began to express publicly their resentment at attitudes of over-protectiveness and the practical domination of their lives and affairs by the hierarchy. A rather modest Woman's Lib mood affected them, so that they at least tried to shed their image as passive, docile, subordinate females. On the whole this was done with much good sense, humour and tact, but there were instances when the message had to be spelt out somewhat aggressively. At one general assembly of French sisters convoked to discuss the affairs of their order, the presiding cleric was told publicly, and not too politely, that his presence was unnecessary and offensive. Most female religious, too, modernized their religious habit and many dispensed with it altogether.

Although there were many who, with the advent of these changes, looked back like Lot's wife in nostalgia, solidified in regret and dissolved into the bitter salt sea of recrimination, criticism and sometimes withdrawal, the changes were usually undertaken with enthusiasm, and strengthened rather than shook the foundations.

One felt, after these 'updating' operations had banished so much of the archaic, pompous, cluttering conventions, like an actor who had previously always played behind a huge masked costume but was now on stage exposed in face and figure. In other words, some of the external trappings had gone, but the romantic role-playing still continued. A nun weaving her way through Liverpool traffic on a Vespa would still consider herself to have 'despised the vanities of the world', according to the wording of her vows. Religious life was still called 'a state of perfection', a 'second baptism', an 'angelic life'.

The real challenge to such romanticism came, not with adaptation to modern conditions, but with an allied, though distinct and deeper movement called 'renewal'. This was and is the re-examining of the very essence and relevance of religious life in the light of a renewed theology. The radical cries for a 'worldly' Christianity or for an anonymous, religionless living of the gospel were not only confusing but shattering for many a pious monk, nun, sister or brother. They were either siren voices to be shut out, or challenges to return, in the very name of Christ, to the world once forsaken in the desert of vows and prayer and asceticism.

Moreover, the sober statements of Vatican II declared with all the weight of hierarchical authority that the perfection of holiness is a universal vocation, demanded of and possible for all, and not merely for the *élite* in convents and monasteries. These statements lit, as it were, so many fuses, creeping doubts, which sooner or later triggered off an explosive rejection of religious life by those who had embraced it as the exclusive means of heroic sanctity.

It was no longer a question of facing the incomprehension of non-believers or the indifference of nominal Christians who seemed to worship at the shrines of money, power and permissiveness. The righteous thrive on such opposition. *Now* the deepest kind of doubts were being sown by many intelligently committed Christians, and even by members of religious orders themselves.

About four years ago an article entitled 'Are Nuns Necessary?' appeared in a magazine devoted to the study of religious life. In the long run, the author held, convents are as foredoomed as the Latin Mass Society, for holiness is going to be understood in secular terms. Moreover, modern, as opposed to mediaeval woman no longer has to choose between being a breeding agent in marriage or being a career woman in some form of previously convent-dominated work such as educating or nursing the poor. 'Is there any relevance, philosophically, theologically or sociologically in the renewal of religious life? . . . Should it not be left to die gracefully and piously in the odour of cloistered sanctity which gave it birth?'[1]

The question, of course, applied to all forms of religious life: male and female; so-called 'contemplative' and 'active'; monks, nuns, canons, canonesses, friars, brothers, sisters. Are any of these necessary? Strangely enough, many of those who eventually left religious life in disillusionment were the ones who first tried desperately to prove its objective necessity. Christ founded it, some said, in his call to the few to be perfect, leave all and follow him. The church founded it, said others, to possess at least one utterly pure form of Christianity. The world needs us, affirmed another group, for who else would keep alight the flame of contemplation and completely disinterested universal availability? But Christ did not found religious life. 'To be perfect' simply means to be as Christ, like the Father in unconditional justice and mercy. To leave all and follow him was at first a specific invitation by Christ to share his itinerant ministry and was understood later, by the writers of the gospels, as a general call to the inner freedom required of all men in order to walk in the way of love. Nor did the official church authorities found religious life. Even the Vatican recognizes it as a free prophetic phenomenon and assumes only a rather external role of guidance and encouragement, seeking to discern the authentic and condemn the false. As for 'pure Christianity', only Christ has lived that. Certainly religious have been and are invaluable to the church in her ministry of proclaiming the gospel in all sorts of ways. But this ministry does not demand religious life. A person can be a priest, a deacon, a deaconess, a catechist, parish worker, missionary, preacher or prophet outside the religious state.

23

Not even on the level of prayer or selfless activity for others is religious life singular or indispensable. At the present time centres for meditation, meetings for ecstatic Pentecostal prayer, Bible-study circles, gospel and life prayer cells, creative liturgy groups are proliferating outside the convent or monastery. The Samaritans, the Simon community, Oxfam, Help the Aged, race relations work, community development centres, not to mention secular schools, hospitals, social welfare departments and political organizations, all offer possibilities for self-giving to the world's deprived which are equal to any within a religious community.

Of course there has always been a defensive insistence within religious life that it cannot be justified or adequately evaluated solely in terms of its works. Not every religious, therefore, felt threatened by the thought that the caring professions and the multiple forms of religious ministry could be realized outside the monastic way of celibacy, poverty and obedience.

Religious life has always explained itself in terms of holiness, love of God and love of others in him. Indeed, reactions ranging from reverential awe and extravagant praise to instinctive prejudice and mocking contempt have been and are accorded to religious because of this claim that their life is essentially a striving for perfection, a specializing in the things of the Spirit.

These extremes of honour and derision are largely independent of the actual virtues or vices observed in religious. They result from the very *idea* of being in some way separated, for spiritual purposes, from the ordinary mode of living in society and from the very idea of devoting much of one's time and energy to specifically religious activities like prayer, worship and study of the scriptures. They result also from the notion of 'consecration'. When a person publicly, that is formally and liturgically, dedicates himself by a vow to God in celibate love, for the specific purpose of growing in holiness, he is regarded as 'consecrated', set apart and belonging in some special way to God. It is hard for the one involved to avoid a sense of spiritual superiority, particularly when he is told, as in a recent book by a Roman Catholic priest, that an 'ontological' change is effected by this consecration, automatically endowing his every subsequent act with a 'plus value'. Françoise Vandermeersch, writing about nuns in 1967, said that 'that which everybody will experience at the resurrection is what is now pursued and already attained through religious consecration'.[2] No wonder Sean O'Casey could speak of 'the quiet indestructible conceit of the monk'.

Of course, the terms 'consecrated' or 'holy one' have often been intuitively understood in a very sensible way. It is rather like calling the Sabbath holy or sacred. In fact, the Sabbath is no more holy or sacred than any other day – for every day belongs to the Lord. The Sabbath simply makes explicit, in its rest and worship, what is implicit even on dreary Monday mornings – that we are not slaves to work and worry but have been made 'a little less than the angels' and must never lose the vision which transfigures the sordid everyday – the liberty, fraternity and equality of God's kingdom come on earth. Similarly, religious may be thought of as no more holy or sacred than anyone else, but as those who make explicit, by their more continually conscious immersion in the 'things of the Lord', that being-for-God which is the inner truth of all created reality.

Such reasoning comes close to the nerve-centre of the present debate on the necessity of religious life. What many religious cannot accept is the conclusion that it is not necessary to enter the monastic state in order to belong undividedly to God or live unconditionally the holiness that is 'a life time's death in love'. They feel that it threatens their identity and *raison d'être*, just as many other believers suspect that it challenges them to total integrity in their own religious commitment.

There is so much confusion over the relevance of religious life for human and Christian fulfilment, i.e. holiness, that it is necessary to spell out the implications of commonly held theories. The confusion seems to stem from differing conceptions of the nature of holiness. Even within the one religious tradition, holiness means different things to different people. Obviously, if two religions can be proved to be radically different, then their concept of holiness will have dramatically different implications.

In a religion or philosophical system in which the highest good consists in the suppression of desire (as would seem to be the case in Buddhism), or in total passivity to a pre-determined fate (which would seem to be the case in certain forms of Stoicism and Gnosticism), the measure of holiness might indeed be that of renouncement. Renouncement of possessions, of self-will, of the normal expressions of sexuality, these might well be considered necessary to reach the heights of a holiness identified with detachment. Dualism, the opposing of spirit and matter, occurs again and again in religious and philosophical thought. Hermann Hesse, in his novel *Steppenwolf*, sums up its effect on our self-understanding.

> Man is nothing else than the narrow and perilous bridge between nature and spirit. His innermost destiny drives him on to the spirit and to God. His innermost longing draws him back to nature, the mother. Between the two forces his life hangs tremulous and irresolute. What is commonly meant by the word 'man' is never anything more than a transient agreement, a bourgeois compromise.[3]

Avoiding compromise implies for Hesse, as he makes plain in *Narzis and Goldmund*, choosing one of two seemingly impossible alternatives. Either you choose to break out of convention and the pallid search for mental truth, to seek, like Goldmund, Dionysian ecstasy through lust, violence, art and nature. Or you take the way of the saint, typified by the monk, Narzis, who by the slow death of asceticism goes beyond fleshliness, rises above 'time and the world, money and power', pain and passion.

Despite what is held by many Christians and non-Christians, however, it must be affirmed that Christianity does *not* envisage man's possibilities as *either* angelic *or* animal, or as necessarily a 'bourgeois compromise' between the two. The love of wisdom and the love of man are *not* mutually exclusive. In Christianity the transcendent and the immanent are paradoxically united so that man cannot approach God through bypassing the human and natural, creation and community. But we cannot bear much of paradoxical reality, and tend to make contradictions out of aspects of human existence that should be held in the creative tension of bipolarity.

The Christian aim is one many-splendoured thing – that man should be, become, fully man. That, however, means to become the image of God, not the God of philosophers and scholars but him who is revealed in Jesus Christ as 'fire, joy, love'. The fundamental simplicity of the Christian message is that all human living finds its meaning and fulfilment in love and through love. Christ reveals to us the only way to achieve such love – by a movement analogous to dying and rising, losing one's life to find it. From experience most of us know the truth that Christ taught and lived, that life lived in communion can only be attained by a painful breaking through the narrow prison of selfishness, greed, egomania, which separates and divides individuals and groups.

If this is our faith, then religious life as we know it, characterized by voluntary celibacy, by varying degrees of asceticism, by much liturgical prayer, must answer for itself not only at the bar of psychology, but even more at that of the gospel. For if Christianity sees man as essentially an embodied spirit and calls him to be the image of God in love and relatedness, how can the choice of celibacy, apparently saying 'no' to a fundamental aspect of embodied love, be an authentic mode of Christian existence? It is not by refusing a human partner that a man becomes a partner of God, but by living in the love that is given to all men by him who is jealous, not of Eros, but of sin, the adoration of self. And how does a man or woman escape self-idolatry in the solitude of celibacy? As for organized asceticism and constant praying – what have these to do with Christian holiness? It is not immediately apparent that they are anything more than distractions or even distortions of our faith. For it is not our sacrifices that God wants but our justice, not our constant mouthing of 'Lord, Lord', but our daily conversion to the will of God which is that man should be liberated personally and politically, individually and socially. Far from being regarded spontaneously as a very pure form of Christian living, surely religious life should be regarded with an initial suspicion. Unlike John the Baptist, Jesus and his followers were reproached for their apparent lack of asceticism. The Son of Man came 'eating and drinking', loving and being loved, praying not that his disciples might be taken out of the world but that they might be saved from the evil one whose home is an empty heart and pharisaical perfectionism.

These are the kind of questions that began to trouble many religious in the self-searching that became so widespread in orders and congregations after Vatican II. They are, of course, the kind of questions that should always be put to candidates in the long period of waiting, testing and preparation prior to their final commitment within a community. Doing this has the happy consequence of reducing almost by half the number of possible religious. Happy, not because there is a population explosion in communities, but because so many of those who desire to be consecrated to God in this manner are motivated by a less than Christian spirituality. They are not convinced that holiness is a universal vocation and a universal possibility. Nor do they perceive that the monastic way is at least as ambiguous and full of dangers as other ways. There is the danger of the heart drying up, the danger of 'religion' replacing faith, the danger of spiritual pride, the danger of ignoring the radical secularity of the Christian vision. They so often think in terms of escaping the influence of evil, forgetting that they bear its source in their own hearts. The best in tradition has always held that the facing of all such demons is one reason for a novitiate.

It was only to be expected that those who encountered such challenges for the first time, whose security in their state of life depended to some extent upon a belief in its superiority, began to suffer crises of identity and meaning. It need hardly be said that crises of this sort were most acute in the Roman Catholic orders and congregations. Anglican and Protestant religious communities could not have come into existence in the nineteenth century without struggling with the objections to monasticism that were so closely associated with the origins of their churches' independence from Rome in the sixteenth century. The Reformers, Luther, Melanchthon and Zwingli had condemned both the practice and the principle of the religious state as blasphemously claiming to be a 'second baptism', as denying the fullness of the Christian life to seculars, as claiming justification by works rather than by faith, as contrary to the freedom of the gospel and the duty and right of man to marry and have a family. Melanchthon wrote in 1521 that 'there is no Christian sphere where Antichrist is more able to reign than in monastic servitude'. In England, Henry VIII's dissolution of the monasteries was motivated by political and economic rather than theological considerations. Nevertheless, there must have been enough evidence of greed, idleness and arrogance in monasteries, to say the least, for the suppression to have been possible and for the general lack of sympathy in England towards the religious state which even today is quite widespread.

Both Anglican and Protestant communities, however, have their problems, one of whose principal roots is, perhaps, archaism. Many of the Anglican communities seem to have come into existence strongly affected by a kind of romanticism regarding mediaeval monasticism. They did, perhaps, look upon themselves as the heirs to that great tradition, albeit purified of whatever was 'Romish, superstitious, fanatical', and reproduced as much as possible the ascetic customs, ways of common life and worship of the mediaeval orders. This may be less true of the Protestant religious communities, but here the danger may be that of too rigid an identification with the basic assumption of the great sixteenth-century Reformers. This seems to have been that religious renewal can only be possible by a return to the authenticity of the primitive church. The very notion of reform seems to absolutize origins. There may then be in both traditions the danger of that archaism which looks for its inspiration in the past and thinks in terms of reforming rather than of transforming religious life. Our present historical consciousness makes us very aware that every era, that of the primitive Christian community as well as that of mediaeval Catholicism, is culturally conditioned. In relation to the kingdom of God it will always need to 'come of age'. At the same time, though, one cannot forget that Roger Schutz, prior of Taizé – perhaps the most famous of Protestant-originated communities – has always insisted on the historical, limited and provisional character of every expression of the kingdom. In general, however, my relatively limited experience of Anglican and Protestant communities suggests an inspiring awareness of the need for continued *moral* renewal, but little sense of the need for radical *structural* renewal.

Objections – how good they are for us all! It is only when we are free enough to call ourselves and the most fundamental aspects of our existence into question, to interrogate our motivations, to evaluate the objects of our choices and commitments and their effects on our lives, that we begin to live and love more wholly, more enthusiastically, more unselfishly, and perhaps in a revolutionarily new manner.

# NOTES

1. W. MacSweeney, 'Are Nuns Necessary?', *Doctrine of Life* 6, Autumn 1968 (supplement), no. 23, p. 171.

2. F. Vandermeersch, *The Life of a Nun*, Geoffrey Chapman 1967, p. 55.

3. Hermann Hesse, *Steppenwolf*, Penguin 1965, p. 74.

# 3 Solitary Refinement

But what exactly, readers may be asking, *is* this life that is under discussion? What are its aims and how are they achieved? How did it begin and develop, and what are its basic characteristics? A phenomenon almost as old and as widespread as Christianity itself cannot be defined exactly or described comprehensively. A glance at its history shows that it comes in many different shapes and sizes. The diversity of forms is as wide as that between the Carthusian monks, silent and solitary in their cluster of hermit cottages, and Mother Teresa with her sisters hastening to be involved in areas of acute human distress and disaster, caring for leprous outcasts in Calcutta, refugees from Bangla Desh or strife-ridden Ulster Christians.

The variety is so great that terminology is something of a problem. It is more than a question of correct labels. A monk by any other name might not in fact sing as sweet – particularly if he were named a cleric regular: say, a Jesuit, who is not trained to sing splendid liturgies in monastic choirs but to teach and preach, to humanize and Christianize society. Strictly speaking, monasticism is only one branch of religious life. In church law, monks and nuns are distinct from friars, brothers or sisters, canons and canonesses regular, religious clerics and so on. One needs some Heinz-sight to take in such a variety of blends! There are, of course, definite bases for these technical distinctions in the life-styles of the different branches of religious life. It has been said, for example, that where the monks ran away from men, the friars ran after them. In the past, indeed, monks and nuns, whether or not they specialized in contemplation, have been characterized by living and working within the monastic house and grounds, whereas members of other communities, friars, brothers, sisters, religious priests, are to be found out in society involved in a number of tasks, secular and ecclesiastical. But at present, in the Roman Catholic communities at least, especially in those most ardently undertaking their own renewal and adaptation, there is some confusion of identity, almost amounting to a crisis. Vatican II asked religious both to return to their sources, the fundamental inspirations and aims of their founders, *and* to adapt themselves to present-day culture and needs. Now the attempt to follow these two directions, intended to be complementary, and to help each religious family to find its own identity, is in some places tending to tear communities apart.

One striking example is the monastery of Boquen, a small abbey hidden away in the fertile and pleasant countryside of Brittany's Côtes du Nord. It was no more than an almost invisible heap of stones when a Trappist monk, Dom Alexis Presse, went there alone, not simply to rebuild it from its ruins but to reform Benedictinism by returning to the life-style of its origins. For ten years he had been abbot of the Trappist monastery of Tamie. There the style of life seemed to him to have ceased to reveal its primitive inspiration. As a historian he knew that the original ideals were as obscured with modifications and additional observances as the stones of Boquen were then overgrown with weeds. After some years, the abbey of Boquen was restored and a primitive observance of the rule of St Benedict (even the twelve-hour day) was revived. At the same time a great simplicity and an uncluttered pattern of life was sought. And yet Dom Alexis told his nine brothers that the experiment was to some extent a failure. The original inspiration had not only to be discovered but also to be re-expressed in new forms. 'We have either to vegetate or adapt.'

The task of such adaptation he passed on to his successor, Dom Bernard Besret. This young and highly gifted monk had been an 'expert' on religious life for the bishops of Vatican II. Under his influence the abbey changed radically. Whereas before the monks had been silent, white-robed figures, rising at 2 a.m., chanting many offices in choir and disappearing from public gaze into the shadows of the cloister, they now dispensed with monastic garb, monastic enclosure and special times and places for monastic silence. It became possible for anyone to enter and share the whole life of the community without questions or conditions. Men and women, married and celibates, other religious and priests did indeed come and associate themselves more or less closely with the poor, prayerful life of the abbey. Instead of being the traditional 'power house of prayer', it was becoming an exciting centre of a critical, lyrical and political Christianity.

But Boquen's transformation did not go unnoticed. Dom Bernard was deposed as prior and higher superiors came hurrying from Rome to investigate and to ask, fundamentally: 'Is this still a monastery?' 'Yes,' replied Dom Bernard, 'if by monastery one understands a centre of edification for the people of God . . . No, if one understands a way of life based on a retreat from the world and from men, expressed in institutions of a bygone age.' The higher superiors may have found at Boquen a handful of brothers living in authentic poverty (i.e. in great simplicity, sharing and hard work), in celibacy understood as a particular way of love for God and man, in mutual obedience, in prayer, in many ways of studying the word of God, in complete absence of worldly ambition. But they found, too, the city overlapping into the desert in the person of politically committed students and middle-aged married couples; secularity sweeping the cloister corridor in the persons of mini-skirted young women and blue-jeaned boys. So the question in the order as a whole was, and still is: have Dom Bernard's adaptations gone so far as to lose for his abbey the solitude and contemplative withdrawal from the world which St Benedict himself sought when he left his studies in Rome to live in a desert cave in Subiaco?

The question is not whether this kind of direct and somewhat overwhelming contact with seculars is a good thing for all religious, but whether or not it harmonizes with the particular values and life-style of *contemplative* monasticism. It is a question which, as several contemplative communities realize, is not really asked while it remains theoretical. So one finds that in France, America, Holland and even in England, the strict enclosure of monasticism is no longer practised. Sometimes this merely amounts to a patronizing permission for a guest to have a meal in the monastic refectory. More often it is a genuine sharing of life, of worship, contemplation and apostolic concerns in which the religious are enriched as much as seculars. One can even find previously cloistered Dominican nuns or Trappist monks working in a secular factory or office. On the other hand, many congregations of 'active' sisters or brothers are restructuring their life in such a way as to allow far more opportunities for solitude, contemplation and liturgical worship than previously. So it would seem that distinctions between the different branches of the life are blurring at the edges, or at least shifting from a communal style to an individual choice. Some feel this to be a betrayal and a frustration. They desired initially not only to live in consecrated celibacy, seeking the kingdom of God within a worshipping and sharing community, but *also* to specialize – perhaps in contemplation or study or some apostolic ministry – and desired a lifestyle that would help them to do so. It is rather like an artist marrying an artist, hoping to share not only a conjugal but an artistic life, when suddenly one partner becomes a business director and expects the other to read the *Financial Times* and to entertain business colleagues. Eventually, some communities will become sufficiently flexible and unencumbered to permit a diversity of life-styles to individuals or small groups within the one community. Others will undoubtedly try to redefine themselves, recreate their own particular identity and concerns and live them organically, but permit individuals to pass easily from one community to another when their personal evolution requires it. What is important is on the one hand to avoid a kind of apartheid system, as if the Christian life were not mysteriously whole in each individual, and on the other not to reduce the exciting variety of religious gifts to a grey sameness.

In the East, Christian monasticism has never been divided into different orders and congregations, nor has a distinction been made between enclosed and active communities. There are autonomous monasteries or groups of monasteries in which a monk or nun is regarded above all as a specialist in prayer. Here a member may live as a hermit or in community; may equally well be active outside the monastery caring for the spiritual, pastoral or political needs of the people or within it in artistic, intellectual or manual work.

However, whether in the East or the West, behind this amazing diversity are there not certain common and specifying elements that identify the religious life, that enable this whole phenomenon to be filed under one name? A few years ago the answers would have been swift and simple, but now they require, if not subtlety, at least much qualification, weighing of words and, above all, the right context. On the whole, religious are not eager at present to state immediately what differentiates them – if anything does. Doing so in the past has often meant forgetting the end through absorption in the means. 'What is important,' declared Dom Bernard Besret, 'is not to be a monk but to be a man and, if possible, to be a Christian.' A glossy American magazine asked 'What is a Sister?', and was answered:

> A Sister is simply a person who has chosen to make herself available as Sister instead of as wife and mother. She is certainly not different from other women except as people are naturally different. I think she should be poor, chaste and obedient, but then I think that all Christians should be that . . . I agree with St Irenaeus that the glory of God is man fully alive, and that whatever promotes life and growth is good.[1]

Language is important, particularly to those who are struggling to be dissociated from what they consider to be a false image. Why should the term 'religious' be used for this group of people, many of whom would want to be regarded as no more religious and no less secular than any other intensely Christian person? Besides, various pejorative connotations cling to the concept of religions. It is seen as the endeavour by ritual, pietism and taboo to grasp and manipulate that which can only be graciously given – communion with the divine. Associated as it is with 'churchy' paraphernalia, it almost seems to be opposed to the main concerns of the modern man of faith for mysticism, love and passionate striving to better the world. Even in its more precise philosophical sense, connoting any activity of prayer or worship which makes explicit man's relation to God, 'religion' should not be the defining term for the individuals or groups under discussion. For them, as for every Christian, this activity is only one part of life. For some it may occupy more time than for others. But it would be a betrayal of Christ to make 'religion' in its technical sense an absolute. Because what mattered to him was the quality of human existence, that we should be as free as possible, brothers and sisters to each other and children of the Father. Even where religion is meant to refer to a whole life lived as worship in its secular as well as its sacred activities, and not to over-concern with religious practices, it does tend to make an *élite* of monks and nuns, sisters and brothers. They should not claim to be anything more than one instance of a worshipful life. So in this book 'religious life' is used for want of any better expression, and particularly to avoid the fearful Roman expression 'states of perfection'. It will be seen later that 'monasticism' might prove a useful general term rather than one denoting a particular branch of the religious life.

In any case, the first thing to be affirmed about religious life is its relativity. What is important is neither to be married nor to be monastic, but to understand and progressively realize our call to a full human existence. As religious we are not an echelon above the human but, we hope, on the way to deepening our humanity. Secondly, we must all be convinced that the only crucial commitment in realizing our human vocation is the com-mitment to live 'in Christ', who offered himself as the Way, the Truth and the Life. If a man or woman becomes a Christian, it is as an explicit acknowledgment that Christ in his vulnerability and his victory, his dying and his rising, is the shape of man's endeavour to become himself. Not that the Christian community is the exclusive or perfect milieu of life in the spirit of love and truth and reconciliation. St Augustine said: 'Many are of God who are not of the church, and many are of the church who are not of God.' Wherever there is genuine striving for human justice and love and peace, there is the kingdom of God which Christ proclaimed and which must be ever more effectively realized on earth in the 'full and free life for which persons thirst, the universal fraternity to which society aspires'.[2] It is the vocation of the church to be a proclamation and an instance of this kingdom, and a religious community has no higher calling. It is not above or outside the whole Christian community, but is one cell of its body. The life of a monk or a nun is not in itself a super-Christianity, but one way of striving daily to understand and live the basic movement of Christ's life.

If there are a variety of ways of living the Christian vocation, it is because there are a variety of human conditions that may be lived 'in Christ'. And underneath the outward paraphernalia of religious life, vows, prayer, work, cloister and costume, is simply a human condition, sexual solitude, become a human adventure because it is entered into for its own paradoxical possibilities of communion, freedom, integration of the self and productive living. 'You should have said "entered into for the love of God", ' some will object. Yes indeed, but then one cannot be authentically given up to the love of God without finding oneself and one's fellow men, just as one cannot authentically give oneself up to the love of one other human person without (perhaps unknowingly) finding God and the whole universe 'of mice and men'. 'To have turned away from everything to one face is to find oneself face to face with everything,' wrote Elizabeth Bowen. The one face towards which a religious is turned is undoubtedly that of Christ. But in this face shine not only the beauty and terror of God, but also the beauty and terror of the world of persons and things that God is making and loving. Not that seeking God necessarily implies living in celibacy, for 'whoever abides in love abides in God'. Nevertheless, historically and psychologically this is where religious life originates – as an impulse towards sexual solitude, because for some individuals the experience of the kingdom is such that it renders marriage, in Fr Schillebeeck's words, 'existentially impossible'. It does not render human love impossible; rather, it makes it imperative, but it opens out ways of love and structures of human communion alternative to those of marriage.

If it is truly Christian, celibacy is not an abstract ideal or the result of contempt or spiritual pessimism towards sexual passion, any more than marriage is an abstract ideal or the result of contempt for the religious dimension of life. Monastic celibacy is the effect of a spiritual experience of the kingdom, having its own psychological and physical repercussions, just as marriage is the effect of a psychological and physical experience of another possessing its own spiritual depths and horizon. The effects of such celibacy are not the withering away of sexuality and passion, but the development of these from a pole or axis complementary to that of marriage. For what is meant by the kingdom is not some Platonic realm of ideas or pure forms. Nor is it an extra-sensory heavenly Jerusalem, glimpsed through the mists of time and space, in which the celibate plays the exile and refuses to sing the earthy songs of human love. The kingdom is *this*

37

world seen in the light of that relationship with God which underlies and penetrates all life and all relationships. It is, as it were, the name of the game of living, striving, loving, a name which signifies that these realities have both an immanent divine source and a transcendent future towards which they must be kept open. The celibate should know very well that erotic love is a way in to deeper union with God and to what Dante called a 'universal good will'. It remains, however, psychologically imperative for him to live towards the world and persons, to love and serve them, from the pole of union with God, rather than the other way round. And if the human emptiness that follows is lived as a form of waiting upon God, it should not be too surprising that God 'who fills the hungry with good things' will ensure that 'he who sows in tears will reap in joy' – the joy of Christ living in the heart by faith and impelling that heart to give to others as much love and life-giving acceptance as it has received.

In principle, if God in Christ becomes the lode-star of a person's heart, it is impossible *not* to sail into the deep waters of human love, even if it is celibate. Yet it is true that in practice one encounters some religious who are not opening out in prayer, tenderness, self-knowledge and social concern, but are nothing more than human prayer-wheels and/or cheap labour for church and state. However, that only proves that if one cannot find in solitude – of whatever form – an alternative way to insight and communion, then one should never have started on the journey at all. Bernard Moitessier, in contrast to Donald Crowhurst, found that sailing the world alone was not so much a test of endurance as a quest of enrichment. He could not come back to land for the very joy of his strange existence. Crowhurst died in the despair of a man, perhaps materially, but certainly psychologically, ill-equipped for the venture. Here is a parallel whose relevance is evident: there are, sadly, dead or dying persons in religious life as well as those who are intensely alive and whose growth in vitality and joy is not *in spite of* but *because of* their seemingly negative form of life. One is reminded of Arthur Koestler's remark to Anthony Grey that not everyone could be so unexpectedly enriched by solitary confinement as they – he had seen individuals becoming 'nastier, bloodier' because of it.

Here we may recall the statement of the sister who said: 'I believe that whatever promotes life and growth is good.' But it is recognized far more widely now that many religious have made romantic mistakes in their quest for a life-giving environment, and monasticism spells for them the opposite of an 'escape to fulfilment'. They are being positively encouraged to leave – if it is at all possible for them to find their bearings elsewhere with confidence and strength.

Bernard Moitessier's experience of sailing the high seas alone can be applied to religious life in another way. Anyone who listened to and watched his own televised account of the journey could see that the relation between his solitude and his enrichment could not simply be regarded as 'sublimation'. 'Sublimation is a process said to be the deflecting of libido towards non-sexual aims. Thus an athlete may impose a temporary continence upon himself in order to achieve greater speed or strength or whatever. But the centre of Moitessier's interest was not in the achievement of a goal extrinsic to his solitude, for the sake of which he stoically endured it. His solitude was not for the sake of undistractedly concentrating his forces on overcoming the hazards of the voyage and winning the contest. On the contrary, he was certain of being the winner when he turned back to the ocean – and for what? Not only to keep on sailing but to enjoy for as long as possible the fruits of solitude itself. For him it was a way of more intense living, a more vivid appreciation of the small and particular: his tobacco or coffee, hungry seagulls, playful dolphins, and of the immense and universal: the changing faces of the sky, the fearful storms followed by serenity and sunlight, the awesome black nights in which he learned that 'there is nothing to be afraid of'. When he re-read his favourite novels he did so with a level of insight not previously attained. And even the human communion which he appeared to be renouncing was deepened for him. Let him who hears understand – and if not, admit a deplorable lack of imagination.

It is probably just this lack of imagination that leads people to grant a spurious justification to religious celibacy by referring to the possibility of sublimating sexual energy into spiritual or social 'good works'. Monks and nuns fret not in their narrow cell of sexual confinement – this argument goes – because, presumably, they have substitute satisfactions: lepers to nurse, children to teach, spiritual books to read and write, monastic brothers and sisters to befriend chastely. It is a rational explanation, but somehow it is wrong. *Alternative* ways of love are not quite the same as *substitute* satisfactions. The alternative way of insight depends on fidelity to the inner solitude itself and not on its suppression – as the beautiful and terrible experience of the desert depends on its still being a desert. It is here that is grounded, in a manner alternative to experiences of intense solidarity, the possibility of loving oneself and others as oneself. It is precisely when you are close to feeling superfluous because your existence is not confirmed by a total communion with one other person that you may see how trivial yet irreplaceable is your own and every other being. The solitude itself is a way of connecting with the acknowledged or unacknowledged solitude of everyone. And when you are aware, however obscurely, that your own ultimate significance comes from a relation deeper than any particular relation – an absolute and individual relation with God – and that, moreover, this is a relation that you share with every creature, then you are at least on the way to understanding and living solidarity at its deepest. That does not mean loving everything in general and nothing in particular. The Jesuit, Teilhard de Chardin, wrote in *The Phenomenon of Man*:

> As such the collectivity is essentially unlovable. That is where philanthropic systems break down . . . It is impossible to give oneself to an anonymous number. But if the universe ahead of us assumes a face and a heart . . . then in the atmosphere created by this focus the elemental attraction will immediately blossom.[3]

We shall be developing later the implications of this claim that it is possible to live solidarity from within solitude. Here it is important to see that while religious life is not totally defined by sexual solitude, 'for the sake of the kingdom', it is very much tied up with that. There are obviously many forms of the single life which draw their inspiration from Christ's words: 'There are eunuchs born that way from their mother's womb, there are eunuchs made so by men and there are eunuchs who have made themselves that way for the kingdom of heaven. Let anyone accept this who can' (Matt. 19.12). It should be noted that Matthew, ch. 19, sketches some implications of the kingdom for human relationships as expressed in sexuality, power and possessions. It is in the light of the kingdom that men see that their deepest bonds are, to use St John's words, 'not of blood, nor of the will of the flesh, nor of the will of men, but of God'. In this inspirational light, rather than through the force of the law, enduring love in marriage is, Christ affirms, possible – in spite of difficulties. But in this light, too, Christ counters the cynical suggestion of the disciples that it might be better to remain unmarried with the affirmation that love in celibacy *is* possible. Indeed it was for Christ himself, who had no wife, no kinsmen, in a sense, other than God's own bride: humanity itself.

> His mother and brothers now arrived and, standing outside, sent in a message asking for him. A crowd was sitting round him at the time the message was passed to him: 'Your mother and brothers and sisters are outside asking for you.' He replied, 'Who are my mother and my brothers?' And looking round at those sitting in a circle about him, he said, 'Here are my mother and my brothers. Anyone who does the will of God, that person is my brother and sister and mother' (Mark 3.31).

This passage and Matthew 19 are probably the best hints to be found in the gospels on what religious life is or should be all about. It is an attempt to weave a whole pattern from the one golden thread of our spiritual unity, our shared destiny as children of the Father, as members of one another in Christ. This may help us to distinguish it as a spiritual gift from the various forms of ministry – particularly from the ordained priesthood which in the Roman Catholic church is so associated with celibacy. Religious life is not in itself in the order of ministry, though its members may and do participate in any form of ministry, including that of the ordained priesthood. In itself, religious life pertains to the order of holiness, the *subjective* holiness, the 'priesthood of the faithful' which the ministerial priesthood exists to serve and stimulate. In 1965 Pope Paul VI rightly said of religious life: 'It must be holy . . . it must either be holy or it must not be', and in 1967: 'The fullness of love – for God, for Christ, for the Church, for every human being. It is this love-character which gives finality . . . to the religious consecration.' It strives to attain this finality (with varying degrees of success and a measure of failure) through a celibate love which develops into a whole life-form with personal, social, political implications and is expressed in a life of prayer, communion and apostolic service.

By contrast, the finality of the priesthood is the pastoral service of God's people, ministering to them in the name of Christ the Lord, the *objective* holiness of God's word and sacraments, striving to gather them together in his unity and send them into the world as his prophets. The rationale of celibacy in each case is in relation to the finality of each project – and these differ. In the case of the priest, celibacy has to be linked to his role as pastor and living sign of Christ the Lord, the servant and head of his church. Not even the Roman Catholic church tries to make out that celibacy is *intrinsically* connected with the priesthood. Neither historically nor psychologically is it the basis, the originating impulse of the priesthood as it is of religious sisterhoods and brotherhoods. It was not until 1139 that celibacy became obligatory for all priests of the Western church, and that went very much against the grain, since the law only resulted in widespread clerical concubinage until the reforms of the Council of Trent in 1563. Until quite recently its rationale was predominantly in an Old Testament notion of cultic purity – abstention from sexual intercourse rather than from marriage was really the aim. Indeed, Luther and Calvin quite rightly castigated the church for thereby equating physical passion with sin and defilement. Nowadays it is more in fashion to justify the law by talk of the 'availability' given a priest by celibacy. But, of course, it requires little imagination to understand just how unavailable a person can be who is struggling to cope with an imposed continence! The priesthood is a sacred *ministry* whose members may live in any life-form, including that of monasticism. Monasticism is a *life-form* whose members may adopt any ministry – sacred or secular.

In itself, apart from its specialized reference, this term 'monasticism' is very deeply appropriate for the whole of religious life and helps us to focus on its essential characteristics. It derives from the Greek 'monos' ('one' or 'alone'), and has been used to designate those who retreated into the desert to live the solitary life, those who have chosen to live in the sexual solitude of celibacy and those who, through asceticism, have become *one* in themselves, unified, simplified. St Augustine explains that he and his monastic brethren are called monks because they have become, in their diversity, *one* in heart and mind through the ardour of their one love for Christ. We have here almost a summary of the aims and special means of religious life.

The religious life is a life consecrated to the love of God in Christ and therefore directed to the *oneness*, the growing unification of the self, and to various forms of *oneness* or communion with others. It is pursued, paradoxically, by exploring the possibilities of the solitary life. For whether a religious lives as physically apart as a Camaldolese hermit, as actively involved with people as a Sister of Mercy, or as orientated towards a community as a brother of Taizé, he or she has chosen, or been chosen by, that very deep form of solitude which is celibacy. In conjunction with prayer, asceticism and the motive of growing in Christ-like love, celibacy has been the one constant of this life throughout the centuries and among an immense variety of traditions. Not that celibacy is chosen for its own arid sake. Far from it. It is simply the case that celibacy, like any form of solitude, may be not only a confinement but a refinement. Refinement, not in the sense of some Jane-Austenish style of gracious living, but rather the quality of our potentialities of heart, mind and body as they emerge through pressure and radiate through purification. Kierkegaard says that our will should be so hard that it could cut through a rock and so soft that it could be wrapped around the body of a child. And Dag Hammarskjöld, one of God's anonymous monks if ever there was one, refers obliquely to his 'great loneliness' as a fire burning away dross that he might rise 'in a flame of self-surrender'.

This is not at all to deny that erotic sexual love may be equally powerful in its effects upon the personality and in providing conditions for freedom and availability in the love and service of God and man. That would seem to be affirming the obvious. But it is less obvious that celibacy may be a condition of love and have its own freeing, energizing dynamics for those who, as Christ said, 'can accept it'. However, if celibacy cannot have such a quality, far more persons than the million and a half or so religious in the world would be condemned *a priori* to an unfulfilled existence. For any amount of reasons, millions of people

43

are constrained to live as celibates, that is, outside the intimate companionship of marriage and the full bodily expression of sexual love, for the whole or an important part of their lives. One could say of this condition what Anthony Grey said of his experience of enforced solitary confinement, that 'to gregarious human nature it seems totally repugnant; nobody in their right minds would undergo it voluntarily'.[4] But, of course, people in their right minds have chosen and still do choose a life of physical solitude – just as they still do choose freely a life of sexual solitude. And in both cases the choice has often to do with what Grey discovered in his Peking prison and Arthur Koestler in his hours by the window of a Spanish cell. Grey writes: 'And yet the black negative mud of isolation ... can become the soil for an outgrowth of new perceptions, new awareness. The process of assimilation takes time as the unpleasantness of imprisonment seeps away into a state of freedom.'[5] Koestler speaks of the different meanings of freedom. Paradoxically, its being restricted on one level may lead to its growth on another. For him, imprisonment became an invitation to the inner freedom of being alone, being confronted with ultimate realities and opening out on to spiritual space. It was a 'spiritual hot-house' in which he developed a sympathy with others which he had not previously attained.

One of the reasons for using solitary confinement as an analogy to monastic, or religious, life is the occurrence of these hints by men like Grey and Koestler about its possibilities for developing *inner* freedom and *spiritual* insight. For it must be emphasized, in order to avoid a gross misunderstanding, that the important freedom that is a possibility for the solitary for the kingdom of God is not the merely physical availability or freedom of the single life. It is not so much a question of the freedom to *do* particular things as the freedom to *be*, to love, to relate, to find oneself in a particular way. The way of the uninvolved and uncommitted? No, a way more nearly resembling that of the artist or research scientist – a non-possessive receptivity before the object – that jug upon the table, my own face in the mirror, the mystery of a living cell – imaginative enough for the object to become a presence and yield up something of its significance. Freedom to respond to 'things in themselves', to allow the other to be present as other, is precisely the burden and the joy of celibate love. It is not a different finality from any other kind of love, perhaps, but a different way in. It is not a state but a project, and it can bypass none of the laws of sexual development, of affectivity, of concentration, of domestic courtesy, of our social and political modes of interaction. Indeed, if asceticism has any meaning at all in religious life, it is as the discipline for achieving such freedom and creating community – communion with God, oneself, others, the world – from within celibacy.

So, too, 'spiritual insight' is neither introspection nor that metaphysical reflection for which several ancient Greek and Roman philosophers remained single. The 'monachos', the solitary for God, *may* be introspective and/or metaphysical or neither. His main aim is to know God existentially, to listen to his word spoken not only in scripture and the sacraments but in his own heart, in people, places, events, objects, history – and to respond to that word. Again, it is both an enthusiasm and a slow learning:

> He who for the first time has Thee in his keeping
> is disturbed by his neighbour, or his watch;
> He walks bent over Thy footprints
> as if laden and burdened with years.
> Only later does he draw near to nature,
> becomes aware of the winds and the far distances,
> hears Thy whisper in the meadow,
> worships Thee in song from the stars
> and can never again unlearn Thee,
> for everything is but Thy mantle.
>
> For him Thou art new and near and good
> and marvellous as a journey
> which he makes in silently moving ships
> on a great river . . .[6]

If such fruits of freedom and insight are possible within religious life, then it may be said to be an authentic mode of human existence. It is not automatically good or sacred. But in so far as it is a milieu which helps some people to realize our common human and Christian vocation to the maturity and the many dimensions of love and liberty, then it is a very good thing indeed. Nevertheless, it has to be admitted that it is a surprising

45

choice. For there are other means of attaining its aims, and this route contains risks, as has been suggested. They are risks which are unnecessary except to those who are strangely impelled in the name of their own integrity to live with them and through them. People, however, *are* surprising. Even though most artists, writers, thinkers, for example, may find that economic ease and normal sexual involvements sustain and enrich their particular genius, yet some will find that they compromise dedication. He or she is then impelled, perhaps like Kierkegaard against his will, into the life of an 'outsider'. About a year ago there was a relevant column in *The Guardian* written by Catherine Storr. She spoke of the need in some creative persons for physical solitude and in others for a deeper kind of separateness.

> When they are offered the sort of friendship or marriage which most of us would gratefully compound for, the relationship which includes common interests and affections, as well as the sharing of physical passion, they hold back. They recognize that, if their genius is to have full play, they must be free to listen to its compelling call at whatever moment this comes; they need a sort of isolation and independence which is not compatible with the closest of human ties.[7]

The artist in one of Camus' short stories gives his own hard-won judgment as to the right condition for artistic dedication in one badly written word which is either 'solitaire' or 'solidaire' – solitary or solidary. The point of the story seems to be that the artist needs solitude for the sake of his own artistic solidarity with the world. Far from being mutually exclusive, solitude and solidarity are two aspects of the organic wholeness of any authentic life. We are all of us constituted by the quality of our relationships and we grow in and through them – but it is a unique and fundamentally separate self that grows. Aloneness is atrophy and death without relatedness, which in its turn is suffocation and slavery without its counterpoint. Nevertheless, although they are inseparable, solitude and solidarity, like silence and sound, are distinct, and may constitute different starting points or basic situations in one's life.

It is not only the life of art but the art of living – the exploring of one's capacities for communion with God, with other people, with nature, with beauty and wisdom – that may require some radical solitude as a basis. A very moving testimony to this is

Dag Hammarskjöld's journal *Markings*. Slowly he learned to assume his deep solitude and live it in such a way that it was 'delivered from the anguish of loneliness'. He wrote:

Hunger is my native place in the land of the passions. Hunger for fellowship, hunger for righteousness – for a fellowship founded on righteousness, and a righteousness attained in fellowship. Only life can satisfy the demands of life. And this hunger of mine can be satisfied for the simple reason that the nature of life is such that I can realize my individuality by becoming a bridge for others, a stone in the temple of righteousness.[8]

It was a hunger that he knew would not be satisfied in familiar patterns.

Some have to be (explorers) – because the frontiers of the familiar are closed to them.[9]

He knew, too, that:

My friend, the Popular Psychologist, is certain of his diagnosis. And has understood nothing, nothing.[10]

Hammarskjöld was a professional man, an economist, a civil servant and Secretary-General of the United Nations Organization. His solitude was not therefore of a material kind – it was not isolation. His mysticism was not opposed to his political and social involvements, but rather a dimension of them. 'In our era, the road to holiness necessarily passes through action,'[11] is a remark that W. H. Auden, in his introduction to *Markings*, says would startle a 'mystic monk or nun'. On the contrary, a monk or nun would probably only take exception to the word 'necessarily'.

The very reason for referring to Hammarskjöld in this chapter is to make clear the *kind* of solitude we are positing as central to religious life. The majority of religious live in fraternal communities and are immersed in activities that are often purely secular. One must listen to God's word not only from the song of the stars but also from the sounds of the city, from schools, hospitals, welfare departments, town councils, research centres, racial ghettoes, factories, offices, demonstration marches – from the sounds of persons and groups within and outside the religious house.

For him who has responded to the Way of Possibility, loneliness may be obligatory. Such loneliness, it is true, may lead to a communion closer and deeper than any achieved by two bodies.[12]

47

*May* lead to communion – and on the other hand may lead to a destructive isolationism:

> Your ego-love doesn't bloom unless it is sheltered. The rules are simple: don't commit yourself to anyone and therefore, don't allow anyone to come close to you. Simple – and fateful. Its efforts to shelter its love create a ring of cold around the Ego which slowly eats its way inwards towards the core.[13]

This last quotation may help to explain several other constant characteristics of religious life. For it points to the terrifying dangers of any kind of solitude, physical or psychological. It is only too easy to live religious life as an opportunity 'to sleep, perchance to dream' – and worse. Nature notoriously abhors a vacuum, so that a negation like celibacy, if it is not an alternative way into the understanding and love of reality, will be not only an emptiness but a hell of alienated living. It will necessarily be a corrupt affair of masochistic asceticisms or petty compensations, and indeed of not so petty ones, such as the abuse of power or the accumulation of collective riches.

So it has always seemed essential that what became known as 'poverty' and 'obedience' should be integral dimensions of a celibate existence chosen formally for 'the sake of the kingdom' and approved as valid by the church. These may strike us as being but two more negations, the final walling-in of individuals to a life (or death) of confinement. The terms are perhaps further examples of the naïveté of self-communication that we have already referred to. They are part of the 'private' language of convents and monasteries, each term possessing a field of meaning that presupposes familiarity with the monastic tradition. Outside this tradition, the word 'poverty' connotes economic deprivation; 'obedience' at least suggests the contrary of self-determination – to *vow* which would be regressive for an adult. In reference to religious life these terms are meant to indicate essential conditions and expressions of the love, freedom and insight which are its aims. To be free *for* the things of the Lord – contemplation, forgiveness, peace, justice, fraternal love – is conditional upon being free *from* cluttering possessions and egotistic ambitions. It means struggling a whole life long against being dominated by the desire to possess and being possessed by the desire to dominate. Moreover, all the talk about the kingdom, the gospel, love, is just rubbish unless the lives of individuals and communities express concretely that material goods need not be the source of division and inequality and that man's will for survival, more, his will to 'rise and shine' in life, may be integrated into a quest for the common good. Obviously, these things are true for everybody, but they have to be made very explicit in religious life because the human loss involved in celibacy can so easily seek its compensations in possessions and power. Who tries to be an angel, as the saying goes, may become a beast. It is not too difficult to see that celibate life in convents and monasteries (especially those withdrawn for contemplative purposes from close involvement in secular society) can become a closed microcosm, introverted and self-concerned. In fact it was only in the Middle Ages, when religious life was in serious need of reform, that celibacy, poverty and obedience emerged as three specific vows.

In material and practical terms poverty means that possessions are held in common in a religious house, distribution being made to each according to his needs. Luxury and superfluity are to be avoided individually and collectively for two reasons. One is that our treasure and therefore our hearts should be in God and in the riches of fraternal love. The second is that sharing must go beyond the community, outwards towards others who are in need. In practical terms obedience is in line with the very root of the word which suggests 'listening to' – listening to the will of God by listening *to* each other and listening *with* each other to its varied manifestations. As such it implies accepting and contributing to the authority of community decisions and aims which may be mediated by the rule and superiors (though some communities have neither). In spiritual and ideal terms both poverty and obedience mean a constant conversion to a Christ-like life. Negatively this implies all the discipline of freeing one's needs from greed and acquisitiveness and one's will from aggression, laziness, self-enclosure. Positively, poverty should be understood as generosity and availability, the possibility of giving and receiving with increased strength and swiftness. Moreover, Prior Schutz of Taizé, in his book *L'Unanimité*, writes:

Today the spirit of poverty demands much more than generosity and detachment. Sharing in the miseries of the world is first of all a sharing in the world's struggle against misery. More than ever

49

before, we are confronted with the question of evangelical poverty in the light of two-thirds of mankind who live in abysmal wretchedness.[14]

The positive sense of obedience is sensitivity and responsibility, the refining of our ability to listen and respond to reality within and around us. What direction is there to be found, what response is there to be invented in every concrete situation, so that the truth may be done in love? That is basically the question of obedience, whether it applies to the individual religious and his or her spiritual, domestic, professional life or whether it applies to the community as such, as a network of relationships and as a body of influence upon its environment.

In sum, poverty and obedience are the way by which the religious ensure that their celibacy is a manner of following Christ, of living his values and his one law of love. They belong to the inner logic of celibacy, if its purpose is that the isolated 'I' should become a 'We' – a mutuality in love. Love of God, it should be specified, but as meaning an *inclusive* love in which the heart is not closed to anyone or anything. 'By their fruits shall you know them.' At its best, celibate life lived in Christ's poverty and obedience does issue in many good fruits. They are evidenced in fraternal love, in contemplation, in the celebrations and lyricism of art and worship, in multiple forms of service to the wider community, and in individual lives manifesting the fruits of the Spirit: peace, joy, compassion, fidelity, courage.

Such a list might seem to suggest that, to extend our metaphor, 'everything in the garden is lovely'. Of course not. Whatever may apply to gardens, human lives are never all lovely. The essences of things may be as sublime as Mona Lisa, their existence as ridiculous as that same lady with a moustache drawn over the lovely smile. When the Dadaists so aggressively made that addition, they were making a comment on human reality as valid in its own order as that of Da Vinci. Much is ridiculous about religious life. Often high pretensions are mocked by the mediocre reality. Generally speaking, the fault now does not lie – as it may well have done just prior to the Reformation – in the moral quality of the lives of individual monks and nuns. Perhaps there has rarely been a time in the history of the church when they were so universally free of corruption. The monastery or convent is quite freely entered and is not a dumping-ground for the disinherited or the maritally unmatched. Its members are chaste and loving, on the whole remarkably free from the consumer mentality, and concerned with alleviating injustice and poverty. They strive to give the best they have to the service of the church and the world with a very unmediaeval abstention from the power game. Yet for all that they are relatively ineffectual as witnesses to the transforming power of the Spirit of Christ. 'Behold I make all things new.' Where in the religious world has all the renewing power gone? Today we need to see new visions, to dream new dreams of human community, to find new symbols in which to celebrate Utopia, new ways of saying yes to life's goodness, of saying no, even with our blood, to society's oppression of its weaker members. Yet in religious life there are but a few individuals and communities that are truly prophetic. Is it fear of fantasy or fanaticism that makes the majority a shade too well-adjusted? It is the same sorry story here as is told ad nauseam elsewhere – in reference to politics, education, family life, racial and sexual inequality and so on. There is a lack of sufficient imagination and courage to change *structures* radically, to invent new forms expressive of new ideas. Christ himself warned that old wineskins would not support new wine nor a worn fabric a new patch of cloth. When sisters made themselves hideous by cutting off a few inches from the veils and skirts of what were often very graceful and becoming costumes, rather than adopt totally secular dress, they unwittingly became a symbol of a far more extensive failure to rethink modalities. In so many more instances there is the same kind of timid, forced acknowledgment of the life's purer beginnings and its contemporary requirements.

This question will be taken up in further chapters, as will be the relationship between the vows and community, prayer and service. Here the point has been to show briefly that the vows are interrelated as three facets of one life-project. Many religious today make only one vow, which expresses a radical commitment to Christ in celibate love, a commitment necessarily demanding a transformed Christ-like relationship to possessions and to power. There is a tendency to avoid using the terms 'poverty' and 'obedience' as being ambiguous and too exclusively negative. But what is more important than the name or the number of the vows is

51

their meaning. The changes and demands for changes in convents and monasteries during recent years have been the subject of not a few articles in newspapers and magazines, and in America, Holland and France they have been given a fair amount of coverage by radio and television. The presentation has often been simplistic, suggesting a revolt against asceticism and strict observance of the vows. At times there has been an extraordinary likeness to the discussion of prison reforms! What is really happening is both deep and complex. In relation to the other apostles, St Paul said of himself that he was 'as one born abnormally late'. And in relation to modern culture religious life has very tardily given birth to a new self-understanding in response to the insights of existentialist and personalist philosophy, of psychology and sociology, of revolutionary political analyses of society. Many religious are themselves well-qualified in philosophy, psychology, sociology, political or economic theory. They have tried to apply the categories from these disciplines to their own life, to question it and to give a renewed interpretation to its various aspects. Here are a few titles from fairly recent articles and essays on religious life by religious:

'Protest Movements and Convent Life'
'Freud and Sisters'
'The Burden of Vested Interests'
'Renewing Religious Power Structures'
'Bureaucratic Dysfunction in American Convents'
'Are Institutions Obsolete?'
'Politicalizing the Reform of Religious'

The inter-subjective dimension of the vows; the possible collusion of religious in their attitudes and work with subtle oppressions in society; the psychological mechanism that no amount of charity can or should cover; the important distinction in community life between primary and secondary groups – all these and more are thrown into relief in the healthy penetration of monasticism by modern culture.

The other source of change is not modern at all. It is the effort, an ever-recurring one, to exorcize with the spirit of the gospel the demons of legalism and un-Christian other-worldliness. This other-worldliness is to some extent related to legalism. Both are vocational hazards for the religious, and when they have a hold they gradually paralyse all life and vitality. Legalism meant that celibacy was reduced to a withering preoccupation with safeguarding chastity. Needless to say, the male hierarchy has shown the greatest zeal for safeguarding the chastity of women religious, not only in the enclosure decrees of the thirteenth and sixteenth centuries, but even today. What, one wonders, is Cardinal Antoniutti suggesting in his recent letter to the School Sisters of St Francis, warning them that their new freedom is leading 'to practices that are not only dangerous but a source of scandal, such as late hours, indiscriminate visiting . . . and worse'? Doubtless he will receive a more vigorous response from the sisters than that which the seventeenth-century Madame de Chantal felt able to give the hierarchy during her bid to escape enclosure laws. She wrote to one of her nuns: 'When the good Archbishop speaks to you of enclosure . . . answer him only with your modesty and decorum, perhaps with a little smile . . . that we are daughters of obedience, loving our institute very much, and that this answers everything.' Certainly outsiders could hardly be blamed for thinking that religious had made a vow of frigidity rather than a commitment to communion in and with God.

The dominance of the law also worked to take the life out of the vow of poverty. Poverty became reduced to a system of using money and goods with permission from superiors. The preoccupation with economy worked against the whole aim of the vow. It became sterile in respect both of the individual's spiritual growth and of the transformation of society. Legalism, too, gradually twisted obedience into a destructive docility and an identifying of the will of God with minute rules and human authority.

To be sure, it is unfair to project all the blame upon the hierarchy. Their laws were not even intended to replace spontaneity, vision, inspiration, but to be rather primitive safeguards against corruption by stating clearly the basic minimum conditions for religious profession. If legal reforms degenerate into legalisms that enslave the spirit to the law, if masters become masters and slaves become slaves, it is because of that unacknowledged collusion in apathy, in the fear of freedom and abundant life, which makes cowards of us all.

It is far too simplistic to think that the solution consists in abolishing any and every legal structure in religious life. The origin of the tradition of having some kind of rule or constitution lies not in the hierarchy but in the needs of religious communities themselves. These needs are not the ordering of the domestic life of a group, nor indeed the domesticating of an order. In the past, it is true, rules and constitutions have contained, besides theological principles, a host of prescriptions regarding details of the common life, and thus have been responsible for standardizing and impersonally controlling matters that are relative, essentially changeable and the domain of individual or democratic decision. But even here the pervading intention was that a religious community should be holy in every aspect of its life – or should not exist at all. Thus in the Rule of St Augustine the fundamental law, the ideal, is expressed as follows: 'Above all the reason for your coming together is to live in unity, having but one heart and one mind turned towards God.' This oneness in love, the summary of holiness, was to be translated into the concrete organization of the monastery. All goods were to be held in common, but care was to be taken in their distribution to allow for individual needs. The rule then prescribes for the concessions that may have to be made to those whose former lives were passed in luxury and refinement or to those who are sick. In the same logic it prescribes that clothing should be held in common, and if complaints arise one is to consider that it is the clothing of the heart that matters rather than that of the body. Today hygiene, fashion and psychology may demand other practices than a common wardrobe – but one can still appreciate the basic intention of St Augustine's ruling.

Underlying this whole question of a rule of life, which has been very important in the history of monasticism, is the fact that a religious community is not any kind of free association of persons. It is a free coming-together for a seeking of God in a striving for the perfection of Christ-like love. 'Where two or three are gathered together in my name, there am I in the midst of them.' Nothing matters so much as to ensure by every means possible that religious come together and stay together *only* in Christ's name. They should begin and continue in their lives to attend to him who is in their midst as their inspiration, their leader and their true source of unity. The common good in a religious community is not an insipid harmony of individual interests. It lies wholly in 'the interests of Jesus Christ', in the things that pertain to the Lord, in creative fidelity to his word and to his impelling Spirit. No law can generate such a life, but only the living responsiveness of persons to their situation seen with the mind and heart of Christ. Yet some formulation of aims in keeping with the gospel may well be of help to a community as a criterion of membership and as a constant reminder of the kind of life to which they are vowed.

When a community is beginning – or beginning again, as so many are at present – when it is small and/or gifted with an inspiringly charismatic leader like St Augustine, St Francis, Mother Teresa or Prior Schutz of Taizé, it may find it easy to be both authentic and fervent with few other structures than the shared life itself. Sooner or later, however, there is the problem of the false prophets or the totally unprophetic personalities. The former try to assert their prejudices and the latter to diffuse their mediocrity. The Christ-centred ideal is obscured with deformations or compromise. Moreover, unwritten rules and conventions emerge and begin to take precedence over the only absolute, which is the gospel, the liberating law of Jesus Christ. Lacking any *inspirational* authority of its own, a community is then exposed to the interferences of the hierarchy, which all too often imposes a juridical authority upon them, quenching the Spirit with prohibitions, sanctions, organizational solutions.

At some stage, then, it will be necessary for communities to reflect upon themselves in the light of the gospel and to articulate in this same light their own basic ideals and aims as well as the principal means of achieving them. Call the fruit of such an endeavour what you will – rule, constitutions, norms, directives – none of them are law in an absolute sense. They are or should be references to both the gospel and the particular spiritual gifts that inspire a group of persons to come together in celibate love for the sake of the kingdom. It is of the utmost importance for religious to remember that a rule may work against its own purpose if it ceases to be regarded as relative to the Spirit and therefore provisional. Religious above all should live as a pilgrim people, travelling light towards the Father, flexible in their institutions, unwilling to be burdened with false absolutes. For the kingdom,

55

outside which their celibate lives have no religious meaning, has never fully arrived. There has to be a constant moving on, taking leave of old patterns and evolving new ways of thinking, living and acting.

This is one of the reasons why the Roman Catholic church has asked all its religious communities to redefine themselves, permitting them to abrogate old constitutions and formulate new ones after an adequate time of consultation, reflection and experimentation. The hierarchy reserves to itself the right to approve or disapprove of religious rules. In *principle* this is admissible, for there are endless distortions of Christ's message that claim to be of his Spirit. St Paul warned Timothy to judge doctrines, to see if they conformed to Christ's own words and led to Christ-like living. He warned him particularly against the false asceticism of those who forbade marriage and commanded abstinence from foods. It is necessary to see what kind of motives and intentions are behind religious asceticism. But in *practice* religious may often have to react against the actual exercise of this role of the hierarchy. For it often oversteps its own limits by unwarranted, depressingly authoritarian infringements of the rights of a community to adapt and evolve in the light of contemporary needs and new theological perspectives. When the priests are blind, the prophets must lead them. As it is, religious are far too prone to lose their charismatic dynamism without being further petrified by bullying bishops and interfering Vatican officials.

The most frequent victims of such excessive supervision are women religious. In 1969 the leading organizers of the National Coalition of American Sisters expressed the conviction that it was principally because of male domination of sisters in the church that within a year there were ten thousand fewer sisters in the USA. This is borne out by the fact that so many of those who left formed into new communities which, even if given the approval and help of some bishop or priest, avoided being bound to them or to Rome in any special way. There are about a hundred non-canonical sisterhoods in the United States. They are not given formal recognition as religious, but this matters little, if at all, to them compared with the freedom from bureaucracy and the life-giving experimentation that results.

This tension – between authority and charism – is as good and creative in the church as elsewhere unless, of course, it degenerates into a kind of civil war. Otherwise there is a fruitful dialectic in which the two poles are mutually corrective. Standing back to gain perspective, one can see a common context to the experimenting religious and the cautioning bishops. This is their common concern that religious life should not be an end in itself, remaining in the margin of the Christian community or the human race. Rather, by its vitality and fruitfulness, it must speak a saving word to both and contribute in its own way to bringing about in society the new age, the kingdom of God. The points of tension are, first, that in order to do this more effectively today, many religious see the necessity for a complete transformation of structures, whereas the hierarchy tends to see only the necessity for an inner moral transformation of persons. Secondly, these same religious are very sensitive to the fact that much in their past manner may have contributed to a world-denying vision of holiness, an 'opium of the people' kind of religion. An American sister sketched this as the old image:

Withdrawal from the world to be alone with the great Alone, adoring Christ in the quiet of the sanctuary, uninvolved in the affairs of the secular world, seeking the things that are above in institutions set aside for our own use, lacking knowledge or contact with other religious groups, piling up grace and merit while contemplating eternal truths, uninvolved in current issues, fearing those things that endanger salvation, praying about the human condition vaguely known through family members or church papers, leaving secular matters to laymen, while as religious being involved only in spiritual matters, or in social activities directly under church auspices, awaiting the beatific vision where human concerns fade into nothingness.

In the movement to do away with whatever made religious sacral or separate in dress, behaviour, buildings, places and types of work, etc., the hierarchy sees a danger that religious will completely lose their own identity and have nothing original and radical to contribute to the church and the world. The prophet has to participate with his whole life, and in a manner that has an impact, in a value which society is in danger of ignoring. The church relied on religious particularly to keep alive the desert experience of Christ, to witness to the world that it does not live on bread alone, that possessions and power are ambiguous, that if God does not build the city they labour in vain who do so, that

57

the world can only be transformed in the spirit of the Beatitudes. The hierarchy has a valid point to make, but it usually makes it very badly. It is true that some of the new breed of monks and nuns almost give the impression that 'bourgeois is beautiful'. They are too well-groomed, their houses too well-appointed, their tastes too luxurious. They are as pathetic in their own way as black people for whom integration means espousing culture and values acceptable to white people. But what the bishops fail to understand is that it is not necessary to return to an *outdated* culture in order to safeguard an *alternative* culture. Religious are quite justified in doing away with their separating symbols – habits, barrack-like convents, enclosure laws and the rest. They surely cannot claim a charism of the Holy Spirit to dress and behave in a mediaeval rather than a modern way. But they *have* a birthright, and if they sell it for a superficial acceptability, they will die. Their proper gift is to live out an alternative approach to sexuality, possessions and power which undoubtedly has a social value in widening men's vision. Theirs is a *via negativa* cutting a fissure in the rock of society's normality, helping to develop a sense of what the painter Dubuffet called 'that vaster beauty touching all things, even the most despised'. He said of his art what religious might well say of their lives – that it tried to reveal the beauty of that which convention regards as negative, tried ardently to celebrate 'scorned values'.

Living the scorned value of celibacy has, however, often led religious on their part to scorn complementary values such as marriage. Religiously motivated celibacy has been interpreted as a situation in which one lives 'for God alone'. This implies that others are to some extent divided in their commitment to God, even if living in faith, hope and love. Which is nonsense. One lives for God alone in so far as one refuses to make any created reality absolute. One is removed from idolatry, not from sexuality. God is not one suitor among others for our heart. St Paul was the first to speak, rather confusedly it would seem, about the virgin being 'undivided' in attention to the Lord. Yet elsewhere he affirms that nothing can separate us from the Lord – neither angels or demons, and so, presumably, neither husbands nor wives! It would be clearer to say that every human situation may be transparent of the presence and power of God – the archetypal solidarity and richness of erotic love *and* the solitude, the poverty of celibacy. Religious life is not more a matter of living for God alone than any other intensely faith-filled life. It is, however, a living alone for God – not necessarily in isolation, but in sexual solitude for the kingdom. The unique contribution of such a life, in witnessing publicly to the Christian mystery, is precisely in manifesting the potentialities of such a human situation, potentialities for holiness and its infinitely varied expressions. To enter the desert of celibacy and become there neither an angel nor a beast, neither superhuman nor subhuman, but simply all that it is within one's uniqueness to become – there is the basic charism of religious life. It is a call to conquer man's fear of the desert, to confront its particular dangers and to explore its peculiar possibilities – to make the wilderness blossom, as the scriptures say. When it is successfully lived (and like marriage it *may* be a debilitating failure), it does at least show that extremes – solitude and solidarity – meet. For God, and with him all good things, may be found both here and there – everywhere that the human heart seeks him. If religious life is no more than one way among others of seeking God-centred human love and fullness of life, it certainly is no less.

## NOTES

1. Michael Novak, 'The New Nuns', *Saturday Evening Post*, 1966.

2. 'The Church Today', 9, *Documents of Vatican II*, Geoffrey Chapman 1966, p. 207.

3. Pierre Teilhard de Chardin, *The Phenomenon of Man*, Fontana Books 1965, p. 293.

4. Anthony Grey in *The Listener*, 1 July 1971, pp. 9 f.

5. Ibid.

6. Rainer Maria Rilke, 'Book of Pilgrimage'; this and the other Rilke quotations come from two lectures on Rilke, given by Gabriel Marcel and included in his *Homo Viator*, Gollancz 1951; here p. 231.

7. Catherine Storr in *The Guardian*, 15 July 1971, p. 11.

8. Dag Hammarskjöld, *Markings*, Faber 1966, p. 62.

9. Ibid., p. 68.

10. Ibid., p. 76.

11. Ibid., p. 108.

12. Ibid., p. 107.

13. Ibid., p. 54.

14. Roger Schutz, *L'Unanimité dans le Pluralisme*, Les Presses de Taizé 1966, p. 9.

# 4    To Cut a Long Story Short

A coachload of young people was returning from a day out together. Passing through West London, one of the group cried out: 'Christ is alive and well and lives in Shepherds Bush!' As good a way as any of summing up the Christian mystery. Nearly two thousand years before, St Paul had expressed it both more personally and more universally: 'I live, yet not I, but Christ lives in me' (Gal. 2.20). 'Whoever cleaves to the Lord becomes one Spirit with him' (I Cor. 6.17). 'We are all . . . to become the perfect man . . . if we live by the truth and in love we shall grow in all ways into Christ who is the head . . . So the whole body grows until it has built itself up in love' (Eph. 4.15 f.).

If one is asked the difference between Christian monasticism and the monasticism of other religions and philosophies, the only answer can be 'Jesus Christ'. This means both far less and far more than it is usually taken to mean. Far less, in the sense that Christian religious are not distinguished because they follow Christ's monastic system rather than that of Buddha or Pythagoras, for Christ founded no monastic system at all. He was the catalyst of the new age which he called the kingdom, and to which Christian monasticism gives expression in its own way. Far more, Christians do not understand themselves to be simply living in the shadow of one who died and whose memory they perpetuate. Rather, they are living in the light of the Living One, through whose Spirit they may become, individually and as a body, another Christ. Christians who are religious believe themselves to be giving one kind of response to this Spirit, embodying in a particular way within history the power of Christ the Lord.

It is well known that Hinduism and Buddhism have their monks. The Moslems hold in great honour their marabouts, who live an ascetical and contemplative life. Philosophers have lived quasi-monastically, the most famous example being that of Pythagoras and his circle, whose style of life had much in common with later Christian monasticism. A Jewish sect, the Essenes, withdrew into the desert to live very ascetically, strictly segregated from the non-initiated, devoted to the study and contemplation of the scriptures, having a very monastic organization in their lives and even, at some stage, practising continence.

As the anonymous author of the second-century Letter to Diognetus said, Christians need not be distinguished outwardly from other men in the organization of their family, social, economic and political life. Nor, one may add, need they be distinguished in the outward organization of their monastic life. But Christians should be distinct in *every* context, in virtue of what St Paul called a spiritual revolution that renews the mind (Eph. 4.23). What such a revolution means in general should be clear from the New Testament, for it is certainly not always apparent, to say the least, from the actual lives of Christians. It does involve bringing to every concrete situation a judgment that confirms or rejects existing possibilities or invents new ones, more expressive of the Christian vision.

Religiously motivated celibacy, though rare, is a possible human choice. Christ cannot be said to have founded it, as we saw, any more than he can be said to have founded marriage. Nor can he be said to have founded the ascetical life with all that it implies of detachment in regard to possessions and power, of discipline over the mind and appetites. But in so far as Christ revolutionized man's understanding of his relationship to reality, he revolutionized the understanding of both celibacy and asceticism. If these are to be Christian choices, they must have a Christ-centred motivation and meaning.

So it is not possible to claim that the Spirit of Christ leads us to refrain from the normal expression of sexuality and the normal use of created goods because they are evil and corrupting. That attitude may well belong to the world-view of Greek dualistic philosophy or Oriental pessimism and determine their asceticism accordingly. When it occurs in Christian monasticism, which it does time and again, it is as a perversion. And when a philosopher like Kierkegaard praises the monastery, and particularly its celibacy, as the only valid expression of Christ's 'absolutely absolute pessimism', one can only comment that his error was as immense as his genius. St Paul warned Timothy that those who forbade marriage and commanded abstinence from food ('good things which in fact God intends to be thankfully enjoyed') were 'spiritually seduced'.

It is also totally opposed to the Spirit of Christ to believe that one can climb to the spiritual heights of union with God by discipline and prayers and asceticism. Not even the quality of our moral life, the keeping of the most basic commandments, are conditions for entering the kingdom of God. Rather, morality and, if necessary, asceticism are consequences of finding oneself already there, in the kingdom. Our renewed doing is consequent upon, rather than conditional to, our renewed being – being in the love which is God. We may marry or abstain from marriage, as we may take food or fast, sleep or watch in prayer, have possessions or give them away to the poor. It is not by any of these that we shall be judged. A religious who was most radically ascetic, the Carmelite friar John of the Cross, affirmed that 'in the evening of life we shall be judged by love'. What matters is that all our options should be taken in the light of that love and as a response to it.

These considerations are a necessary preamble to a sketch of the historical origins and development of religious life. For on the one hand, like any human phenomenon it emerges from and is very much influenced by the particular culture of each historical era and diverse geographical and social situations. On the other hand, it should be equidistant at every point from Christ – Christ alive and well and living in religious in so far as they cleave to him and become one Spirit with him.

The story does not begin with withdrawal or flight into the desert. In the first decades after the resurrection and long before the end of the persecution of Christians, there were in very many of the local communities women and men distinguished from other baptized Christians by their particular charism of 'celibacy in honour of the Lord'. These virgins and ascetics at first lived in their own homes and expressed their purpose of preoccupation with the 'things of the Lord' by a life of prayer, a certain frugality, and often by charitable or apostolic services to the community. Theirs was, however, a charism, or gift, distinct from that of the deaconesses and deacons appointed specially for these ministries. St Augustine later commented that the virgins engaged in various works as Christians rather than as virgins.

To understand the motivation and meaning of this virginity and asceticism it is necessary to remember what we have said about taking up existing human options and living them as ways of 'cleaving to the Lord and becoming one Spirit with him'. St Paul had already preached that the option of marriage, as a union in love, is both a symbol and a means of participating in the love between Christ and his bride, the church. So when St Ignatius of Antioch (c. 110–117) writes of those who remain 'chaste in honour of the flesh of the Lord', his meaning is that such celibacy is an alternative possibility of openness to the one love that must fill the whole Christian community. This is what St Augustine later made more explicit by saying that 'the virgin lives in the flesh what the whole church lives in faith' – complete self-giving to the Lord.

Besides more obvious disadvantages, living in celibacy at home under parental authority and, even worse, entering into celibate marriages (which became momentarily fashionable!) brought the danger that celibacy was regarded as a mortification rather than as the point of departure for an original life-form. Separation from both these contexts, and with it the emergence of a stronger identity for religious life, was achieved in two ways. One was the formation of communities by ascetics of the same local church – no physical separation from society, little organization and at first no other authority than their own ideals and union with the local bishops. The subsequent development, particularly by Pachomius, Basil and later Augustine, of this movement, was shaped and dominated by one idea – fraternal love. Its model was the primitive Christian community of which the Acts of the Apostles tells us:

The believers had but one mind and one heart; no one claimed for his own anything he had, as everything they owned was held in common . . . then distributed to any members who might be in need (Acts 4.34f.).

The other movement was the withdrawal of ascetics to the desert. This may have begun as early as the second century, for the persecutions forced many fervent Christians to hide in some way or to face martyrdom. We are told that one Paul of Thebes fled at the age of sixteen from the persecution of Decius in AD 250, and lived alone in a cave of the Arabian desert until a very ripe old age indeed. In fact longevity seems to have been one of the incidental blessings of the desert. Antony, the most famous of the hermits, was said to be over a hundred when he died. Athanasius, who lived with him for a while, wrote his life, and as Athanasius eventually settled in the West he was very influential in spreading the hermit ideal of monasticism there. Antony was born about 251 in Middle Egypt. His sister entered a community of virgins and he went to live as a solitary in the mountainous desert near the east bank of the Nile. The historian Gibbon imagines him as a 'hideous, distorted, emaciated maniac . . . spending his life in a long routine of useless and atrocious self-torture'! Yet from the account of Athanasius, who, after all, lived with him, 'his manners were not rough, as though he had been reared on the mountain and there grown old, but graceful and polite, and his speech was seasoned with the divine . . .' A man who held that 'amiability' was the chief virtue of a hermit and who before dying gave his old cloak to his friend saying, 'Farewell, you who are my heart strings', might not qualify for the drawing room – yet he seems far from hideous.

It was not only in Egypt, but also in Palestine, Syria, Asia Minor, Mesopotamia and Persia, that deserts became the dwelling-places of hundreds and even thousands of ascetics. Like Antony himself, they made contact with fellow-hermits for the sake of spiritual counsel. Gradually groups formed around a charismatic master such as Antony, about whose den at Pispir there sprang up a small village of huts. There was only a loose organization, each man being left very much to his own devices. The spiritual master was rather like a guru under whom one was temporarily a disciple. They ate dried beans, fresh vegetables, fruit and herbs, came together to celebrate in common worship on Saturdays and Sundays and, one eye-witness tells us, 'showed love to one another and towards such as by chance encountered them'.

It is extremly important to note the difference between these hermit groups and the other fraternities. The fraternities in Syria and Persia, as well as those developed by Saint Pachomius (c.

290–346) in Upper Egypt and St Basil (c. 330–379) in Cappadocia, were not groups of individuals gathered round a spiritual master, but communities in which the fraternal relationship came to be seen as an end in itself as well as a support for the individual's contemplative growth. Here was a common life, strictly speaking, in which the brethren were to serve one another and belong to one another, whereas in the eremitical movement, even when communities formed, they were groups of solitaries, needing each other for mutual encouragement and counsel. Everything converged upon seeking the face of God in solitude and prayer. This does not mean that contemplation was undervalued in the one or fraternal love in the other. For both, contemplation was a monk's business; for both, love was the fulfilment of all the law of God. The author of the *Historia Monachorum*, who visited several hermit groups in Egypt in the fourth century, tells us of the solitaries at a settlement called Cellia, where the cells were about three or four miles from each other.

> There is so much love in them, and by such intense affection are they bound to one another and towards all the brethren, that they set an example and cause wonder to all. If anyone by chance should wish to dwell with them, as soon as they hear of this, each man offers his own cell.[1]

But it does mean that there were in fact two different types of community life, of monasticism. The common life was envisaged differently in each, and there came to be correspondingly different emphases in the understanding of celibacy, poverty, obedience, prayer and asceticism.

In the West there has been not only a fusing but a confusing of these two movements, mainly through the influence of the much-venerated John Cassian (c. 360–453). He was a monk who, after ten years in Egypt among the solitaries, came to France (Gaul), founded two monasteries in Marseilles, and then endeavoured by his writings to reform and conform all the other monasteries in the West. For him the only authentic tradition was that of the hermits or semi-hermits. But he imposed the solitary ideal upon the practice of the fraternity. For example, a superior emerged in the fraternity because a focus of unity and an administrative order were needed where there were large numbers. The superior

65

was not necessarily a spiritual master, but a servant and a promoter of communion among the brethren. Obedience in this case was very different from the temporary submission of a disciple to a master, as in the schools of the desert. Cassian fused the two roles so that that of spiritual director was identified with that of superior, and the essentially temporary and highly personal relation between master and disciple became permanent and institutionalized. Eastern monasticism, on the other hand, has not lost even to this day the tradition of apprenticeship to a holy, Spirit-filled man or woman, whether or not he or she happens to be the superior.

Contemporaries of Cassian such as St Jerome, St Martin of Tours and Honoratus of Poitiers were all very influential in propagating the eremitical type of monasticism in the West. Even noble Roman ladies were fired with enthusiasm and followed Jerome to Palestine to found a convent of nuns there about 386. In contrast, another contemporary, St Augustine (354–430), founded three monasteries in North Africa, two of laymen and one of clerics, whose spirit and practice was completely along the lines of the fraternity. Here the fundamental law which was to govern the concrete life of the brethren was that they should have one mind and one heart, turned towards God. For Augustine, in sharp distinction from Cassian, Jerome and Martin, to leave the 'world' was not to withdraw spatially from society but to form part of a celibate community, leading an existence that differed from other men and women because it lay outside marriage and all its social and economic implications. With the hermits, sexual solitude was lived out in physical separation, the better to wait upon God in asceticism and contemplation. For Augustine, it was enough to be celibate and to live in a community of brethren who all had at heart 'the interests of Jesus Christ', where by mutual love and sharing they became 'the temple of God'. Such a milieu would be sufficient to sustain both contemplation and any activity that the brethren might be called on to exercise for the wider community. Augustine, already a monk, became a priest almost against his will, being chosen by the people of Hippo. But he continued his monastic life then and afterwards, when he became a bishop. Life-form and ministry did not have to clash as they seemed to for Cassian, Jerome and Martin – and still do today for those who wish to specialize in the art of contemplation. Augustine's flexible and very fraternal monasticism seems to be as attractive today in the West as that which, developing from the genius of St Benedict in the fifth century, became the norm in Europe for 600 years.

Benedict was born about 480, the son of a Roman nobleman. He became a solitary, but was quite soon surrounded by disciples. Eventually, he organized a monastery at Monte Cassino and there wrote his famous Rule. It is very much in the line of Cassian's thought, yet tempered by Benedict's understanding of men and his knowledge of other sources, including that of St Basil's fraternities. It is understandable that today Benedictines are asking themselves what exactly is the role of the abbot or abbess – is it that of spiritual guide and teacher in a school of disciples, or that of maintaining the fraternity in unity and peace? Happy the community whose abbot or abbess is equal to both! They are also asking themselves about the nature of their life together – is the model a group of hermits round a spiritual father, or a closely-knit fraternity which may not always need a superior?

Benedict is said to have brought two qualities to monasticism which our contemporary prejudices may prevent us from appreciating: stability and order. Let a present-day Benedictine speak for his founder:

In St Benedict's mind, when he placed stability first – as St Francis was to place poverty first and later St Ignatius obedience – are the twin thoughts of permanence and perseverance. The author of the Rule meant his monk to 'make firm his stability' in a single community, that is the community which had received him, tested him and heard him testify by his profession vows that he would live among them. He meant also that a monk should see stability, not as a tomb that walled him up, but as a continuous vibrant striving towards perfection, a school of service and patient perseverance in Christ's sufferings. This means adherence to initial undertakings, loyalty to first loves, filial attachment to the family chosen at the outset. It involves constancy of mind in adversity as well as prosperity, tendency of heart towards incorporation into community life . . . Stability (in relation to persons) brings acceptance, and acceptance response, and response love: and love of the brethren is the law of Christ and the beginning of the love of God.[2]

As for order, the Rule seeks to balance prayer (about four hours a day), study (about four hours) and work (about six hours). Nothing too harsh or rigorous is prescribed by way of asceticism, and the central authority of the abbot is made less absolute by the rule of consulting all the brethren in council and the seniors for less important matters. Candidates to the order must be seen truly to 'seek God'. The community is to be self-supporting economically and guests are to be given hospitality as if they were Christ himself.

Here, then, was a monasticism which by its very reasonableness, its inbuilt tendency to prosperity, was often to become too attractive, too respectable, too successful in worldly terms. The only safeguard was to keep the rule with a fundamental integrity towards its spirit and most basic directions. For if one aspect of such a well-balanced project were to become disproportionate, the whole would be mightily imperilled. Time and again the reform of Benedictinism was to appeal explicitly for a 'return to the Rule'.

Benedictine monasticism spread, for the monks travelled with missionary zeal all over Europe. With it went not only Christianity but the seeds and sustenance of European civilization. None of the reproaches so often made against the hermits applied here. For its convents and monasteries were centres that radiated learning and culture, and where successful methods of agriculture and architecture were innovated and developed.

Such was the influence of Benedict's rule that by AD 800 Charlemagne was to wonder if there had ever been another, and ordered its observance throughout his empire. But it was as much self-interest as piety that led rulers to meddle in the affairs of monasteries. Their schools and farms and the influence of their stability were to be encouraged. By claiming the right to appoint abbots and abbesses, an emperor, king, bishop or nobleman could appropriate a great part of a monastery's goods and revenue. This was to be one of the great scourges of monasticism – manipulation from outside, the appointment of nominal superiors and pressure to make a monastery pay. These factors, combined with the general chaos that followed the invasion of the empire by Normans, Saracens and Huns, account in some measure for the laxity and disorganization in monasteries at the beginning of the tenth century.

In 910 there was founded in Burgundy, very near the present community of Taizé, the abbey of Cluny. Its influence was to become phenomenal: on society, both politically and culturally, but above all on the reform of monasticism and the church. For two and a half centuries Cluny was gifted with remarkably holy and learned abbots. As early as 931 it had claimed absolute independence from secular authority and local bishops. The Pope alone was its protector, and the monks freely elected their own abbot. Not only did Cluny itself make many foundations, but a vast number of monasteries invited its direction, for Cluny was a symbol of spiritual fervour and freedom from outside interference. By the twelfth century it had upwards of three hundred directly dependent houses and about two thousand others living its spirit and monastic customs. Yet already in the eleventh century Cluny seemed, at least to a few monks, to have lost something of the simplicity and balance between liturgy, manual work and contemplation intended by the Rule.

There was indeed a complex problem, which still continues, with obvious differences, in religious life today. It was not so much the absence of personal holiness in the monks as an obscuring of the monastic life by certain developments. Increasing numbers, the ordination of educated monks, the elaboration of liturgy and liturgical art, the secular feudal system of authority, the burden of lordship over estates and properties were gradually deforming the style and structure of the Benedictine way of life.

With the intention of returning to a greater simplicity and poverty, Robert of Molesmes, a Cluniac monk, in 1098 settled with a few companions in the swampy forest of Citeaux, near Dijon. They promised their bishop 'to conform henceforth to the holy observance of the Rule of St Benedict', and eventually developed into a separate religious family, the Cistercians. They had learned the important lesson that their life should not develop blindly, and so they drew up an authoritative interpretation of the Rule, the Charter of Charity, in order that it should not suffer arbitrary amendments and dispensations. They also instituted an annual general assembly of abbots where problems and changes could be discussed and controlled, and stipulated that every abbot should visit his dependent monasteries at least once a year. (A dependent monastery has its own authority but is not completely autonomous.) Simplicity and austerity in their whole life-style, including their liturgy and architecture, characterized the Cistercians. It was – and still is – their aim to live in much silence, solitude and poverty, to be free for contemplation in an atmosphere of complete openness to God. In 1112 a young knight, Bernard, came with thirty companions to join the little group, which was beginning to despair of its own survival. It was the start of an immense development throughout Europe. When St Bernard was abbot of Clairvaux, there were 700 monks there alone.

The writer Thomas Merton, who died recently, was a Cistercian. He was supremely well able to communicate the inner attraction of a life that seems repugnant to many:

> The one who has been found by solitude and invited to enter it, and has entered it freely, falls into the desert the way a ripe fruit falls out of a tree. It does not matter what kind of desert it may be: in the midst of men or far from them. It is the one vast desert of emptiness which belongs to no one and everyone. It is the place where one word is spoken by God. And in that word are spoken both God Himself and all things . . . The monk is compassionate in proportion as he is less practical and less successful, because the job of being a success in a competitive society leaves no one time for compassion.[3]

Merton had at one time thought of leaving his own order for the more complete solitude of the Carthusians. Their founder, St Bruno of Cologne, had in fact once been associated with the small group which later became the Order of Citeaux. In 1084 he and six companions settled near Grenoble in a remote valley in the Alps, some 4,000 feet above sea level, where the climate is cold and the soil poor. In a Chartreuse, or Charterhouse monastery, there are tiny cottages built next to one another around some communal buildings such as the church and library. Each man lives alone in his cottage, where he has a bedroom, an oratory and a workshop. Normally a small piece of walled garden is attached. He receives his one main meal a day through a hatch, except on Sundays and some feast days when the monks eat together. The day is spent silently in prayer, study and manual work. Twice a day and once in the night all gather in the main church for the liturgy. On Sunday afternoons they may walk and talk together, but otherwise the contact between them is limited.

A monk will converse with his prior or novice-master or confessor, and occasionally request permission to receive spiritual counsel from another.

'Christ's poor men who dwell in the desert of Chartreuse for love of the name of Jesus' is how the group described itself in the early years. Bruno had probably no intention of founding an order, but the movement spread, and in the fourteenth century there were as many as one hundred and seven Charterhouses in Christendom. There were nine in England at the time of the suppression of the monasteries. There are Carthusian nuns, too. They originated from a community in Provence, said to have been founded in the sixth century, which in 1151 requested affiliation with La Chartreuse. Although they observe similar fasts and silence and times of prayer, they do not live in separate houses but in adjacent rooms, and take all their meals in a common refectory.

The hermit life had already revived in the West before Bruno. This may have been due in part to the influx of refugees from Asia Minor who, in the eleventh century, fled away from the Turkish invasions to Italy. Surprisingly (or perhaps not?), it has begun to flourish once more in the last ten years or so, particularly in America. In a recent list of new religious communities in the USA, nine groups of hermits were noted, all founded within the last five years. Most live in small cottages in the traditional style, keeping silent and remote, and all support themselves economically, often through literary or artistic work. What is relatively new (but like the primitive situation of the desert) is that they have only minimal regulations, and are willing to share their solitude with outsiders of both sexes.

Individual hermits can be found in the most surprising places. An architect working on plans for the Olympic Games in Munich told me of the pains he and his colleagues took not to sweep away the little house and patch of land occupied by a much venerated hermit. In Paris there is a small house and an ancient chapel, hidden by some trees, in which a nun hermitess lives. The city does not disturb her, although she is known and loved by neighbours whom she meets on the one day in the week when she goes out for Mass and for shopping. The house has a kitchen and one other room where there is a camp bed, a table on which rests an open Bible, a few books, a small stove for burning logs and a large wooden cross on the wall. There is no electricity and no running water, only candles and a large cistern to catch the rain. Yet the place is impeccable, and the nun, a former missionary, is full of charm and common sense, and has evaded all but one interview. Our imagination might picture a life of pleasant ease, but she spends a very disciplined day in prayer, some reading, house or garden work, and earns her living by needlework. It is very important to her to consult a spiritual director regularly and to see her bishop about material matters as well as prayer. Does she see herself in some sort of penitential role for the surrounding city? When asked this question she laughed and protested that if she is solitary it is 'on account of God', and if she is in Paris it is 'on account of his love for its people. As for me, I am very much a part of humanity – of its sinfulness too – and am in no way one of the *élite*.'

Orders like the Benedictines, Cistercians and Carthusians are monastic in the strict and particular sense of the word. The general rule is that activity shall be within the monastery itself and, although Benedictines unceasingly debate the point, there is a tendency to favour physical separation from the rest of society. The Rule of St Augustine has, as we have seen, other emphases, and has been used by a great number of communities. In the Middle Ages there were many groups of sisters living in towns and cities, devoted to nursing the destitute, who lived according to this Rule. The Augustinian community which still nurses in Paris is one of the many still surviving in France. Sometimes these sisters took a fourth vow 'to care for the sick poor', yet, ironically, they may often enough today be found caring for the sick rich in private nursing homes!

Bishops tried to monasticize their clergy by prescribing at least the spirit of St Augustine's Rule: life in common and shared possessions. However, they met with little success. The aim was to render the clergy more equipped for their ministry. Secular priests were often ill-educated men in isolated rural parishes, contributing more to the curruption than to the spread of the gospel. The monks, on the other hand, kept their superiority within the enclosure, tending on the whole to take Cassian's advice: 'A monk must absolutely fly from women and bishops. Neither . . .

72

will allow him once he has become familiar with them to give himself up to the quietness of a monk's cell . . .!' Eventually an order was formed with the purpose of combining parish ministry and religious life, and not surprisingly adopted the Rule of St Augustine. The men were called canons regular – canon meaning at the time simply a priest with a parish, and 'regular' indicating that he lived by a religious rule. They became numerous in England, and were associated with the foundation of such hospitals as St Bartholomew's and St Thomas's in London.

A German, St Norbert, also founded an order of canons regular. As he began in a place called Premontre in France, they are often inelegantly referred to as 'Premonstratensians'. Norbert must have felt that the spirit of St Augustine needed to be strengthened by that of St Bernard, so he added to the Rule a goodly number of austerities borrowed from the Cistercians. This hybrid creation seems to have been fascinating, for at one time it had as many as a thousand abbeys, many priories and five hundred houses of nuns. Yet the canons patterned themselves too closely on the monks. It was not until the coming of the friars that religious moved out into the new urban and university life, that the emphasis shifted from stability to mobility, from celebrating the good news liturgically to proclaiming it pastorally.

There were other innovations in the eleventh and twelfth centuries. The Hospitallers, founded in Jerusalem, provided lodgings for pilgrims and facilities for the care of their sick in the Hospital of St John, previously run by Benedictines. Many crusading knights joined, but unfortunately they were only too ready to use military rather than medical skill on the invaders. The order had a troubled history after this, and eventually in 1530 was granted the island of Malta, where it remained undisturbed until the surrender to Napoleon. In the early twelfth century, nine French knights formed the Order of Templars. Not only did they take the three vows and live very austerely, but they were dedicated to defending Jerusalem against the Saracens. Perhaps the best thing that happened to the Templars was their entire suppression in 1311 by a decree of the church. True, it is impossible to judge them fairly unless one enters into the whole mentality of their time. They were probably as convinced then of the rightness of defending Christians and Christian places from invasion as many today are persuaded that in the struggle against overwhelming social injustice, a Christian's place is with the guerillas. In every age we effectively say to God: 'My thoughts are your thoughts', and in every age we need a prophet to tell us: 'As far as heaven is from the earth, so far are my thoughts from your thoughts, says the Lord.'

Two such prophets in the thirteenth century were the Italian, Francis of Assisi, and the Spaniard, Dominic, a native of Castille. One was a poet, the other a preacher, and both were pre-eminent in openness to God and love of the world. Although both were to found orders that were a radical departure from previous models, yet they were strikingly diverse as personalities. Francis was in love with Lady Poverty and vowed to become identified with her. Dominic was inseparable from his copies of St Matthew's Gospel and the Letters of St Paul, and totally given to communicating their life-giving word. Even today the different emphases in Franciscan and Dominican life are better conveyed by these images than by an account of particular differences in organization and historical development.

'Lady Poverty' is an image with many associated meanings. It is understandable that a young romantic who was preparing for knighthood, when overcome with an experience of God, should interpret his religious quest in terms of chivalrous love. If that were all, the image would be of only passing interest – and perhaps provide evidence for a Freudian diagnosis. The real significance of the image, however, is that for Francis Lady Poverty was *her*self a symbol of God, and of the soul that becomes identified with God. He instinctively recognized and responded to the feminine principle and the masculine principle both in God and in himself. Like the fourteenth-century hermitess, Julian of Norwich, Francis could call God Mother as well as Father. Moreover his tenderness was such that the brethren would call him Mother as well as Brother or Father.

Francis' mystique of poverty was not a revolt against a materialistic society nor a kind of folksy 'return to the simple life'. It was a passionate response to the love of God which he perceived in all creation, and supremely in the vulnerability of Jesus Christ. Francis knew what the poet Rainer Maria Rilke has expressed so beautifully, that God too is poor:

74

Thou too art poor, like the spring rain
that falls like a blessing on the roofs of the town;
and like a wish nursed by prisoners
in a cell eternally deprived of the world.
And like the sick who change their position in bed
and are happy; like the flowers along the railway line
so grievously poor in the mad wind of journeys;
and as poor as the hand into which we weep.[4]

Francis did not set out to be a founder. He had simply left his affluent home, symbolically stripping himself of his fine clothes in favour of a rough tunic, and gone to live alone in great austerity and joyful openness to God. But men gathered round him to such an extent that before he died in 1226 there were at least five thousand friars present at the first General Chapter (and a hundred years later there were thirty times that number preaching all over Europe and beyond). They travelled extensively, preaching and teaching everywhere, in the market places and in the universities, caring for the poor and sick and outcast, living and proclaiming Christ's message of peace, joy, simplicity and love. The consequent necessity of drawing up constitutions and organizing the order was almost beyond Francis. Before he died it was evident that his brethren were developing not only beyond, but away from him – at least from his radical simplicity and material poverty. In time many splinter groups broke off, each claiming to be reformers in the name of Francis. It would surely matter little to the Poverello, the little poor man of Christ, how the different communities of Franciscans are distinguished from each other, as long as it could be said of all of them:

They are not poor. They are only the not-rich . . .
Yet they are purer than pure stones
and like the blind animal which has scarcely begun
and full of simplicity and infinitely Thine;
they wish for nothing, and need only one thing,
the right to be as poor as they really are.
For poverty is a great inner light.

The poor man's house is . . .
poor as the warm poverty of a stable
Yet there are evenings when it is everything,
and all the stars emerge from it.[5]

Dominic, though equally a man of prayer, long vigils and tender love for persons, was, unlike Francis, a great organizer. He founded a new order quite deliberately, and orientated his brethren to respond to the new needs in society which the monks, on account of their particular life-style, and the secular clergy, on account of their general ignorance and isolation, were not able to meet. He already was a religious, more precisely a canon living under the Rule of St Augustine, when, in 1215, he prepared with sixteen companions to start a new community: the Preaching Brothers. The canons tended to be rural and enclosed. Dominic wanted a life-style in which contemplation and celebration overflowed far more extensively into preaching and teaching. He wanted his men to be implanted in the new university cities such as Paris and Oxford, the commercial centres of London and Florence, and industrial centres such as Bruges and Cologne.

Two journeys into France in 1203 and 1205 had brought Dominic into contact with a movement called Albigensianism (from the town of Albi in Languedoc). This movement held a dualistic form of belief, that matter and human passions proceeded from an evil principle. Its proponents were extremely ascetical, very well versed in the scriptures and untiringly zealous to make converts. G. K. Chesterton describes them in his own inimitable way:

> These persuasive pessimists . . . were highly civilised and . . . wanted to destroy civilisation . . . in one sense they wanted to destroy everything. They were not merely in revolt against the Church, but against the universe . . . at any rate the material universe. They believed in the spirit but were undoubtedly pledged to destroy the sun and the moon as soon as was practicable and convenient. They held that our whole bodily existence is an evil in itself, that marriage is bad because it produces children, that sin is not so bad as long as it does not produce children.[6]

Chesterton goes on to say:

> We can imagine men like ourselves persecuting an intellectual perversion like pessimism and wishing to destroy those who wished to destroy the world.[7]

But Dominic, unlike many churchmen after him, wished to do neither. He endeavoured with his companions to present the truth more persuasively than error, and to manifest in his life an asceticism and spirituality born of love rather than of hate for the world. It is interesting that a religious community came into being as set against this negative philosophy, since so many consider that such pessimism is what religious life is all about!

Dominic was gifted in organizing his community which, from the beginning, he structured democratically and orientated towards communication, replacing the monastic emphasis on manual labour with the obligation of systematic study. But his intention was that this communication should be of God's saving word, effected only in the measure that the brethren lived in and from the word:

> Then receiving a blessing let them set out. They shall behave everywhere as men who seek their own salvation and that of their neighbour, as men of the gospel who follow the footsteps of their Lord and speak with God or of God between themselves or with their neighbour.

Like all other religious, the Dominicans hear the word of God from within their whole life-form: in the fraternal love within the community, in the poetry of their liturgy, in their hours of contemplation and study, and in that inner solitude and poverty which is so particularly a mark of religious life.

Both Dominic and Francis founded communities of nuns, but the customs of the time and the church's enclosure law for women religious kept them behind their convent walls, while the friars took the gospel into the streets, towns and cities, to artisans and merchants, to students and philosophers.

For all their inspiring beginnings, by the fifteenth century friars, as well as canons, monks and nuns, were all too often living in flagrant contradiction to their own ideals. There are very many interrelated causes of this decadence, but the principal one seems to be the effect of increasing compromise over poverty. Then, of course, the vast numbers indicate that in the Middle Ages religious life was an epidemic as much as an authentic vocation – which to some degree justifies our being extremely selective today. There were also the terrible consequences of the Hundred Years War and the Black Death which ravaged convents and monasteries as much as elsewhere, and often left the survivors with an inner plague of bitterness and bewilderment. Many efforts at reform were made both by the hierarchy and by the more zealous of the religious themselves. (Pope Paul IV, it is said, simply rounded up the vagrant scavenging monks in Rome and sent them to the galleys!) But when the storm of the Reformation broke in Europe, not only were there many closures and suppressions of religious houses by secular authorities, but numerous individuals and groups simply fell away like rotten fruit. In a sense religious life is indebted to its illustrious rebel, the Augustinian Luther, for initiating such a crisis, for there was little healing or innovation possible without it.

Both were extensive in the sixteenth century. The Carmelite nuns and friars were strikingly renewed by the mystics Teresa of Avila and John of the Cross. Teresa had long been a nun before she became filled with repugnance at her own and her convent's spiritual mediocrity. She was an extraordinary woman who, by her life, her work for reform and her writings, left an abiding mark not only on the Order of Carmel, but on the whole Western church. New communities of men came into being, specializing in nursing or teaching, concerned to give rather than to receive from the poor. Of those which specialized in the priestly ministry combined with religious life, the most impressive and eventually the most influential was the Society of Jesus, founded by Ignatius Loyola (1491–1556).

Superficially it might appear that the Jesuits were simply more modern friars, better adapted for action and mobility, having no special religious habit, not bound to a choral recitation of the office, immensely well organized to meet the needs of the Reformation period. Yet religious communities are far more deeply and subtly distinguished from one another than by such externals. They have different personalities, as it were, and are ineradicably marked by the personal genius of their founder and the pattern of response to God and the world that takes shape in their beginnings. Much is made of the fact that Ignatius had been a soldier. It is far more relevant that he had the temperament of a Basque from northern Spain, the social character of a man of the Renaissance and the spiritual gifts of a mystic.

While convalescing from a battle-wound in 1517, Ignatius underwent a spiritual experience which changed his whole life. Afterwards, he spent a year's solitude in a cave in Manresa, near the hermits of Montserrat. It was not until 1534, after encountering hostility from the Turks in Jerusalem, and from the Inquisition in Spain, where he was imprisoned for suspected heresy, and after studying at the universities of Alcala, Salamanca and Paris, that with six companions he formally vowed to 'renounce the world' for unconditional service to God.

There are apparent contradictions in descriptions of the Jesuits. On the one hand they are said to be fiercely individualistic, on the other to be blindly obedient. The key to some understanding here is first in the particular mysticism of St Ignatius as seen in his *Spiritual Exercises*, which he began on his sick bed, and which are central to Jesuit spirituality. Secondly, it is necessary to appreciate how much Ignatian spirituality was moulded not only by the Basque temperament of the man himself but by the new social era that was emerging during the Renaissance and Reformation period.

The whole object of the *Exercises* is discernment for the sake of authentic personal decision. More precisely, it is the refining of sensitivity and sharpening of perception so that a person may come to know *from within* what is most likely to be the will of God for him in every circumstance. The exercises are not designed to nurture rationality so much as spiritual intuition and discrimination, the ability 'personally to discover the full and real significance of the events of human history and one's own existence' in the light of Christ. In so far as the emphasis is on personal discernment, there is a legitimate individualism; in so far as the aim is ultimately 'to see the Lord in all things' and to respond to the direction of his will, there is a Christian obedience. Now in one sense this is simply Ignatius' development of a very old theme in religious life, but it is a development that strikingly reflects the social character emerging in his time. In *The Lonely Crowd*, David Riesman tells us that the shift from the tradition-directed mediaeval society to that of the inner-directed social character is so great that 'all later shifts seem unimportant by comparison'.[8] The new society was one of such increased personal mobility, expansion, exploration, constantly new situations and problems that individuality of character had to be highly developed.

Ignatius and his companions were to develop a style of religious life in which a person could be part of such a society, exposed to it in a far more open manner than the monk or the friar, yet maintaining 'a delicate balance between the demands upon him of his life-goal and the buffetings of his external environment'.[9] As a secular description of the aim of Jesuit spirituality, Riesman's analysis of the autonomous man seems peculiarly appropriate:

> The definition of the autonomous refers to those who in their character are capable of freedom . . . heightened self-consciousness, above all else, constitutes the insignia of the autonomous . . . His autonomy depends not upon the ease with which he may deny or disguise his emotions but, on the contrary, upon the success of his effort to recognize and respect his own feelings, his own potentialities, his own limitations.[10]

Obedience is no contradiction to such autonomy. It means for a Jesuit, as for every religious, first that his freedom and self-awareness are lived and developed from within the life-form of religious celibacy in a sharing and worshipping community – a life-form he has freely chosen. Secondly, it means that his freedom is directed to accomplishing the mission, the apostolic activity of the Society 'for the greater glory of God'. The Jesuit emphasis upon obedience and the correspondingly powerful system of leadership is to be understood mainly in relation to effectiveness in the tasks or missionary endeavours of the Society. Obedience is one thing in the context of community life and inter-personal relationships where it means mutual attentiveness, loving service of each other and generous care for the common good. It is another matter in the context of a task or function or mission to be accomplished. Here the need is for more than good will and dialogue. The need is for efficiency, and it calls for leadership with real authority and a highly intelligent and precise response to that leadership. It is quite destructive for the one pattern to be operative in *all* contexts, and the failure to make this distinction can be seen in the unattractive rigidity that characterizes the community life of many female congregations influenced by the Jesuits.

The wildest presumptions are made about the so-called 'obedience of judgment' demanded of a Jesuit. It sounds horribly like the plea made at Nuremberg, the denial of responsibility in the name of obedience. In fact it is nothing of the sort. Rather, it is a pointer by St Ignatius to our immeasurable capacity for self-deception in the name of honesty, for rationalizing our prejudices and for instinctively refusing the love of good will to those in authority. A Jesuit has recently explained it thus:

> Obedience of judgement should mean this: that we use all the efforts of our good will to overcome any personal bias and prejudices, and open our intellects to understand the superior's command in the best possible light, give the maximum benefit of doubt to it and the best chance possible of proving itself efficacious. The will is used to bend the perhaps biased intellect, to let whatever truth and good there is appear to the full. It should not be used somehow to twist the intellect away from the truth and reality, to see things as they are not. This would be contrary to human dignity and the inviolability of the light of human intelligence on which the dignity of the person rests.[11]

Moreover, all religious superiors have to be as obedient as everyone else in the community. This means in particular that all the evidence has to be in before decisions are made, and that no decision is valid which falls outside the framework determined for the whole community by its approved constitutions.

One of the dangers in the life of Jesuits is that their activity is so closely bound up with their *raison d'être* that the aspect of fraternal life in their houses often seems neglected. Jesuits themselves can be heard referring to their houses as bed-and-breakfast residences for isolated individuals or for a team, for a work-force rather than for a fraternity. A community might well be a team when it is 'on the job', but surely it is not a team when it is at home. Here it is a fraternity of love with a pattern as different from that of a task-force as a festive dinner-party is from an American 'working lunch'.

In 1967, the Jesuits numbered about 36,000 members. There are now no 'Jesuitesses', formally, at any rate. But for a society whose founder obtained a decree from the Pope that it should not undertake the direction of nuns, the Jesuits have dominated the spirituality of women's communities to an extraordinary degree. They direct retreats, guide renewal conferences, give lectures, write books and articles for the benefit of nuns. Unfortunately, too much of what they write shows a lack of awareness of the difference between the Society of Jesus and the corporate personality of other communities. To take just one example: the highly centralized government of the Jesuits and their vertical pattern of authority are tolerable and productive only when balanced by a system which allows individuals to develop their own potential to the full. Communities of sisters, too, may help their members to realize this potential, but they are still within an oppressive system: managed, protected, dominated and even exploited by the hierarchy and male orders. After 400 years of influence the Jesuits have not helped sisters to throw off such bonds, but have rather contributed to the forging of them; it might be more helpful if they took Urban VIII's decree literally from now on.

Two priests who tried, one timidly, the other valiantly, to break through the imposition by the hierarchy of a strictly cloistered life for women religious were St Francis de Sales (1567–1622) and St Vincent de Paul (1576–1660). A totally contemplative life had come to be considered as the norm for nuns, but this was not out of consideration for their own aspirations, nor out of zeal for the development of the contemplative dimension in the Christian community. Women were thought unable to cope with the temptations they would encounter if exposed to intellectual or moral opposition. Francis de Sales wanted to help the widow Madame de Chantal to found a religious community to be a house of care for girls with physical infirmities, whose members would also go out to visit the poor and care for the sick. He was finally defeated by the objections of the Archbishop of Lyons, backed up by the recent re-enactment of enclosure laws by the Council of Trent. So the 'Visitation Sisters' became stay-at-home nuns.

M. Vincent avoided the legislation by instructing his sisters not to call themselves 'nuns'. He was therefore able in 1633 to found, with Louise de Marillac, what is now the most numerous religious community in the world: the Sisters of Charity. They number about 45,000 and until recently were universally recognized by their wide, white 'butterfly' bonnets. In the early days they took private vows and lived a community life of prayer, but in accordance with their founder's instructions they were a group

> who have no monastery but the houses of the sick, who have for cells only a lodging or the poorest room, whose chapel is the parish church, who have the streets for cloisters. They are enclosed only by obedience, they make the fear of God their 'grille', and they have no veil but their own modesty.

In time these sisters came to wear habits and live in large convents with private chapels and a certain amount of enclosure. Yet they have never swerved from their dedication to the care of the orphans, the aged, the incurables and the destitute. One cannot help thinking, however, that if they had not adopted the more conventional modes of religious life and become heavily institutionalized, they would now be able to meet the needs of the 'new poor' more quickly and imaginatively, and lead the way where so many secular bodies operate with more slender resources.

Even before the Sisters of Charity there were small local groups of sisters who did not observe the enclosure rules, but in no case were these recognized as religious communities. Such juridical nonsense was ended by the French Revolution, the secularization of church property in Germany and the suppression of religious institutes in Latin countries, which swept away many of the old orders. While the church was thus under attack, new communities proliferated, for the most part active groups responding to local needs: teaching or nursing sisterhoods and brotherhoods, or communities of missionary priests. The nineteenth century saw the development of a swarm of new institutes of a similar nature and also the return of the old orders to some of the countries from which they had been expelled,

As we have seen, the nineteenth century also saw the beginning of a revival of religious life in both the Anglican and the Protestant churches. In February 1841, Pastor Vermeil wrote to a French Protestant, Catherine Malvesin:

For many years now I have entertained the idea of reviving – under another name and without the superstitions with which they are tainted – religious orders of women to care for children, the sick and old people.[12]

In November a house was opened in Paris and the sisters were named deaconesses to emphasize the services that would make them acceptable. Although the deaconess ministry had already been revived, Mlle Malvesin's community is significant because she clearly desired from the beginning to lead the religious life. A deaconess or deacon is a person called to exercise a particular office or service or ministry in the name of the church and, like the rest of the clergy, is ordained for this by a bishop. As we have seen, all kinds of activities and ministries may be an essential part of the life of a religious or a community. But the religious vocation cannot wholly be defined by such service – as is the case with the vocation of priest or deacon. There are more than 40,000 Protestant deaconesses today, only some of whom are also religious. Mlle Malvesin's community, now known as the Reuilly deaconesses, had to bear with a kind of persecution from their own church in their early years. It was only after the Second World War, when new religious communities emerged in the Protestant churches such as those of Grandchamp, Taizé and Pomeyrol, which were quite distinct from the diaconate, that they were able to develop openly all their founders' intentions. They are consecrated to God in celibacy, community of goods and mutual obedience, and describe themselves as 'A community of prayer dedicated to the One Love, assembled in the liturgy, clothed in the constant care for other people. A community of service in the living movement that leads from God to other people and from other people to God.'

At the beginning of this century there was a general reawakening in the Reformed churches to aspects of the Christian life that seemed to have become obscured. A great need was felt to develop more than a humanitarian ethic – a need to revive the sense of the transcendent and the idea of community worship in liturgy and sacraments, to have places of spiritual renewal in prayer and fraternal love. Out of this need several religious communities were born, the most famous being that of Taizé, founded by Roger Schutz, a Protestant who had chosen for his university dissertation the study of St Benedict and the origin of Western monasticism. Taizé is a hamlet in Burgundy, standing directly between the two great centres of mediaeval monasticism, Cluny and Citeaux. Here Roger Schutz bought a house in August 1940 on the feast of St Bernard, that twelfth-century monk-extraordinary. Today there are over seventy brethren at Taizé of many different nationalities and of different religious denominations, Roman Catholics among them. Schutz took the best from the monastic tradition as a whole, but inspired it with his own prophetic openness to the needs and insights of our own time, with his passion for unity and reconciliation in the church and society, with his hunger and thirst for the concrete possibility of freedom, equality and justice in the world. Every year more than 400,000 people come to Taizé for a few hours, weeks or months. Many are young folk – 6,000 from all parts of the globe gathered there last Easter. Here Christianity is most unmistakably and radiantly *seen* to be what it is – a community of love, peace and joy, of lyricism and beauty in worship, of openness to God and to all men, of passionate concern for economic and political justice.

Perhaps the most needed lesson of Taizé for Anglican and Roman Catholic communities is the concrete expression of pluralism within unity and of creative flexibility within the fundamental continuity of monastic commitments. 'Uniformity,' writes the Prior, 'creates an appearance of unity . . . Unanimity supposes a pluralism of personal expression.'[13] He warns the brethren that only if all share together in continual renewal will the community avoid a deadening conformism and the settling into permanent moulds. At Taizé there is a constant reappraisal of the brethren's forms of response to God and to the world, an amazing inventiveness, a sense that everything except the infinitely small centre – total commitment to Christ – is provisional.

In the Church of England at present there are about sixty-seven religious communities, very closely resembling, on the whole, their Roman Catholic counterparts in organization, vows, aims, rule and constitutions. Already in the seventeenth century, Anglican voices declared that monasticism should have been purified rather than amputated. Proof of nostalgia can be found in the extraordinary experiment at Little Gidding by Nicolas Ferrar and his 'family community'. Ferrar (1592–1637) had travelled and encountered monasticism on the continent. His whole household of thirty people – parents, children and grandchildren – began to live a quasi-monastic life: matins at 6.30 a.m., compline at night, meals in silence except for reading, care for the poor and needy, meditation on the scriptures and, of course, a life of work, self-education and recreation.

Monasticism, properly speaking, was only to appear in the Anglican church in the early nineteenth century. At this time there was a profound renewal in the Church of England springing mainly from what is known as the Oxford Movement. Like the Oxford Movement itself, Anglican religious life was regarded with some suspicion – acceptable only if useful in producing 'good works'. But the object of the women who took the first steps was more than to band together as Victorian Lady Bountifuls. A

Miss Marion Hughes had told Dr Pusey, a leading representative of the Oxford Movement, of her desire to be dedicated to God and to be vowed to his love in celibacy. She took a private vow in the church of St Mary the Virgin, Oxford, receiving holy communion from Dr Pusey. This was in 1841, but it was eight years before Miss Hughes was free from caring for her parents and could join a community – by then Anglican sisterhoods had been founded. Between 1845 and 1900 there were over forty such foundations, most of them fairly alike, resembling the Sisters of Charity in giving themselves to admirable and varied work for the poor. From the beginning, the heart of their life was thought to be liturgical prayer and the fostering of a contemplative milieu. Some chose a way more completely directed to such worship and contemplation, not without arousing suspicion and alarm among the Victorians, for this above all smelt of Romish superstition and the socially-useless monasticism of the basket-weaving St Antony! Today contemplative communities of the Church of England are among the most flourishing and vital of their orders, and at least one of them – the Sisters of the Love of God – has nuns who live in hermitages in Staplehurst, Kent.

It was not until 1866 that the first male religious community among the Anglicans began. In that year Richard Meux Benson and two other priests took life-vows of poverty, chastity and obedience in each other's presence as mission priests of the Society of St John the Evangelist, based in Oxford. Their main apostolate was preaching missions and taking retreats, and the foundation of similar communities followed. Perhaps the best known are the Society of the Sacred Mission at Kelham, Nottinghamshire, and the Community of the Resurrection at Mirfield, Yorkshire.

There are also more specifically monastic orders of men in the Anglican communion, such as the Servants of the Will of God in Crawley Down, or the Benedictines of Nashdom Abbey. Immediately opposite Nashdom there is a retreat house owned and run by the Sisters of the Cenacle, a Roman Catholic community. Between the two is a wonderful interchange which results in mutual respect and participation in various aspects of each other's life and work and worship. In fact, it is among religious of different denominations that the absurdity of disunion within the

Christian church is most apparent. For the essential object of religious life is not to know about, but to become Christ. Its deepest aspiration is summed up in the words of the mystic friar, St John of the Cross: 'I do not want the *thought* of you, my God, but you.' And at this level the images and formulations which divide us give way to the love which unites us.

## NOTES

1. Rufinus, *Historia Monachorum*, ch. 22.

2. Editorial to *The Ampleforth Review*, Spring 1971, pp. 1, 2, 5.

3. Thomas Merton, *Disputed Questions*, Hollis and Carter 1961, pp. 197, 200.

4. Rainer Maria Rilke, 'Hymn to Poverty', quoted in *Homo Viator*, Gollancz 1951, p. 236.

5. Rainer Maria Rilke, 'Hymn to Poverty', ibid.

6. G. K. Chesterton, *Generally Speaking*, Methuen 1937, p. 158.

7. Ibid., p. 159.

8. David Riesman, *The Lonely Crowd*, Yale University Press 1965, p. 13.

9. Ibid., p. 16.

10. Ibid., p. 259.

11. W. Norris Clarke SJ, *Woodstock Papers*, v. 96, 1967, p. 520.

12. G. Lagny, *Le Reveil de 1830 à Paris et les origines des diaconesses de Reuilly*, Paris, Association des Diaconesses 1958, pp. 42 f.

13. Roger Schutz, *Unanimity in Pluralism*, Franciscan Herald Press, Chicago 1967, p. 14.

# 5    Kind Love both Get and Give

There is a widespread suspicion, possibly supported by evidence, that religious replace 'love' towards their fellow humans by 'charity', that is, by a discarnate benevolence which cares for and serves others not for their own sake but as a means of self-perfection, or as an occasion for helping God to mend and manage the world. This may indeed be a vocational hazard for religious because they are not committed exclusively to any one person. But it is far from the ideal or from monastic policy, unless Plato rather than Christ is taken as spiritual guide. A rather stupid and arrogant explanation of religious celibacy current today asserts that it *is* a commitment to love, but 'universally' rather than 'in particular'. It is stupid because love does not exist without particular objects – persons called by their own name, known and desired for what they are in their own irreplaceable particularity. It is arrogant because *whoever* is visited by love has the heart extended incalculably and experiences something of what Dante, on falling in love with Beatrice, called 'a universal good will'.

Two things should be made clear at the outset. One is that religious talk a great deal about love because they understand it to be the name, the nature, the power of God. Christ made it clear that to choose God is not to choose a discipline or a morality or a special way of worshipping. It is to choose life rather than death, and this life is identical with love: 'We know that we have passed from death to life because we love the brethren.' But religious most frequently talk as if love were an undifferentiated, univocal activity. Fortunately, the reality is less dull, and ranges from efforts to tolerate the repugnant and care for the needy to friendship, affection and passionate attraction.

Secondly, it is not to be denied at all that in convents and monasteries there are not only frequent failures in love by the best people, but characters who are consistently unloving, selfish – even cruel and contemptuous. Voltaire described convents as 'places where they come together without choosing each other, live together without loving each other, die without regretting each other'. A caricature, indeed, but not so unintelligent as to be altogether unthinkable. However, surely the same words could be applied to some marriages. The point is that you do not define something by how it fails, but by what it intends.

Yet what could a life of worship and service of God in so-called 'consecrated celibacy' intend other than a pious refusal of the invitation to human love? Some answer, it is hoped, has been given in previous chapters. Today one can hardly hope to be believed in affirming the incomparable pleasure and transforming power of physical sexual love in its fullest sense, and yet denying that this is the *only* dynamism that totally opens the heart to love or its *only* authentic expression. That, however, is what has to be said to make any sense of religious life as a possible mode of truly human communion. And it has to be said because that is what is felt and experienced. The inner source and ultimate direction of all love and of all forms of communion are, the Christian believes, far deeper and wider than natural affinity, mutual attraction, sexual desire and common interests, just as they are wider and deeper than blood, nationality, race, colour or creed. These bonds are not pale, unsubstantial reflections of the reality. They are, they participate in the reality, but they are neither its first nor its last word. That word is God's creative love for us, prior to all other bonds, empowering them, surpassing them. It is a love which, if we allow its power to work in us, should abolish all tests of acceptability, all frontiers and passports to our hearts. For it means that we all belong to one another and are members of one another.

True, this is a dream, utopia. But it is God's own dream for us: 'That all may be one, Father, as you are in me and I am in you.' What else is the holiness which is the ideal of religious life, if not the growth of a God-centred love for all things and for all persons? What else is the finality of celibacy, poverty, obedience, if not to live in a developing openness and self-giving to others which has no other *raison d'être* but Christ's good news that we are to become one in God? If God is understood as he whose 'centre is everywhere and whose periphery is nowhere', and if a person is dedicated to him, not only in faith but in the flesh, as it were, mysteriously unable not to offer him the gifts of personal affectivity, possessions, time and talent, then that person is called to a human approximation of God's love which is centred everywhere and nowhere bounded. It means in practice that, negatively, however real and acknowledged are the links of family, friendship, sexual desire, you refuse to be bounded by a total belonging *on this basis*. It means, positively, that you endeavour to centre the love and tenderness you learn through these natural relationships upon each person and event in which you are involved. Christ commanded us all, in one way or another, 'to be generous as the Father is generous who makes his sun rise upon evil men as well as on good and sends his rain upon honest and dishonest men alike'. The project of love in religious life is a kind of parable of that. Voltaire was right in saying that religious were together without choosing each other because, delightful as it is when attraction strengthens our faith in the loveability of others, the basic idea is to deprive no one of whatever creative acceptance and warmth we are able to offer. This is what is meant by the statement in Chapter 3 that the freedom of the 'solitary-for-God' is not so much directed to doing particular things as to being, relating, loving, in a particular way.

It may be objected to this fine talk that religious blatantly contradict such ideals by hiding themselves away in their monastic ghettoes and at times in an extreme physical solitude. Yet surely it can be admitted with Martin Buber, apropos of hermits in particular, that 'the life of dialogue is not one in which you have much to do with men, but one in which you *really* have to do with those with whom you have to do. It is not the solitary man who lives the life of monologue but he who is incapable of making real'[1] the relationship with whatever and whoever he encounters. Buber wrote that he knew people absorbed in 'social activity' but who 'have never spoken from being to being with a fellow man'.[2] A Trappist hermit was asked quite recently whether he were not living a completely self-centred life. He replied that he was trying to lead a God-centred life and that only the love, the unquestioning sharing of himself and his poor dwelling, offered to those who for one reason or another came to him, could prove that this opened rather than closed the personality.

As for those 'ghettoes' – convents, monasteries, religious dwellings – they are in intent communities and schools of love. Where better to express, to learn and develop the God-centred love which is professed and which could very well be nothing more than priggish nonsense? They are intended to embody that sharing of affections, of possessions, of time, talents and freedom which form the content of the vows of celibacy, poverty and obedience. The following text of the commitments made at profession in the Taizé community expresses this intention well. The prior, representing the community, questions and the novice answers.

Will you, through love of Christ, consecrate yourself with your whole being to Him?
I will.
Will you henceforth fulfil the service of God in our community, in communion with your brothers?
I will.
Will you, in renouncing all ownership to property, live with your brothers not only in the community of material goods, but also in the community of spiritual goods, striving for openness of heart?
I will.
Will you, in order to be more available to serve with your brothers and to give yourself completely to the love of Christ, remain celibate?
I will.
Will you, in order that we may be but one heart and one soul, and that our unity of service be fully realized, assume the decisions made in community and as expressed by the Prior?
I will.
Will you, always discerning Christ in your brothers, be watchful with them on good days as well as bad, in abundance as in poverty, in suffering as in joy?
I will.[3]

Very often it is only during the public liturgy of a profession ceremony that outsiders, relatives and friends begin to understand that the community a young person is entering is something more than a huddle of old maids or bachelors, something more than the bleak proximity of individuals singly dedicated to God, living together as so many parallel lives which never intersect and fuse only in some far-off heaven. In one convent of sisters, Augustinians, living in London, the novice, during the ceremony of her first temporary commitment, is publicly addressed by the Director of Novices as follows:

> Sister X . . . the holiness to which God calls all his men is a self-giving love creative of community.
>
> A Christian is one who believes that Christ is the ultimate pattern of such love and that the Spirit is the power by which all men may be one, because through his Spirit we ourselves live the very life of Christ in free obedience to the Father and joyful self-sacrifice for each other.
>
> But the Holy Spirit gives to the members of the Christian community a diversity of gifts by which to realize this holiness in love: some through marriage, some through the single state in the world, and some through life in a consecrated community such as ours. In our life, celibate love, sharing and mutual obedience are the special gifts of the Spirit, the particular ways in which a person expresses the reality of the kingdom of heaven on earth.
>
> It is now two years since you officially asked to share the community's life as a novice, that is as a beginner and as a learner, seeking God within our fellowship of praise and love and service. You have learned above all by giving yourself generously, so that together we have been able to say: 'How good and how sweet it is to live together in unity, having but one mind and one heart turned towards God.'
>
> Do you now feel called by God to bind yourself to the community by a promise of fidelity to its ideal i n preparation for your life-consecration to him by vow?

Here, in one of those moments when a community solemnly and publicly articulates its nature and its aspirations, it is quite clear that to be turned towards God in a radical commitment to him is simultaneously to be turned towards our fellow-creatures. There are not *two* directions to the religious vows – one vertical, towards God, the other horizontal, towards his world of persons and things. The very covenant that a religious makes with God, expressed in the threefold vow, which is for the sake of communion with God, is simultaneously a covenant with that world, and first with that small part of the world in which it is given to him or her to live – a particular religious community.

Some of the rules or directives of religious communities express this very strongly. The School Sisters of St Francis, based in Wisconsin in the United States, have this to say of their vows:

Let us, by living the vow of celibacy, consecrate ourselves to Jesus Christ, to make his mission our own, to extend our love to all men, to show, by living together in love, the goal of his redemptive plan.

Let us, by living the vow of poverty, manifest our unity in Jesus Christ and our dedication to the proclamation of the kingdom, joyful in the Father's love and care for us, stripped of everything which separates us from the poor – whether it is self-righteousness, prejudice or rationalization, identified personally and communally with the values of Christ.

Let us, by living the vow of obedience, make ourselves believable witnesses of Christ's mission by deepening our love of the Father who sent us his life-giving Son, by serving the church in making effective Christ's risen dynamic presence among men, by listening to the Spirit urging us to live in unity with all men.

Nor is this a modern up-dated version of religious life. If we examine the very earliest documents relative to the first attempts at an organized religious life, writings which may loosely be called the 'Rules' of St Pachomius and St Basil, we find that the central perspective around which everything else is ordained is fraternal love. In the first collection of Pachomian rules there is no allusion to ascetical practices such as fasting, watching in prolonged prayer, silence, mortifications, although these may have been part of the life. The whole preoccupation is with the quality of relationships in the fraternity. Pachomius simply quotes the scriptures: 'Love is the fullness of the law' (Rom. 13.10), and Basil weaves many similar texts into his recommendations: 'By love in the Spirit, serve one another'; because each brother is a member of the one body he should neglect nothing that concerns the common good. Obedience and poverty are not separate here, but the concrete expressions of such love. Basil describes obedience as surrendering oneself and one's members to the good of others out of love in Christ. For Pachomius it means mutual service and utter truthfulness in all one's relationships. To teach his first brethren what religious life was all about, he would accomplish all the material services himself because, his biographer points out, his disciples had not yet reached that degree of perfection in which they became servants of one another. For both, the model of the common life was the primitive Christian community described in the Acts of the Apostles, so that for both poverty consisted in calling nothing one's own, but sharing all things as an expression of oneness of mind and heart in God.

It will be remembered that parallel to the Pachomian type of fraternity there was an extensive development of a semi-eremitical monasticism. Here there was no common life in the sense of living under one roof with daily meals, worship and work in common. But there was communion. Love, not asceticism, was the primary value. Observers have left us accounts of the hermits' arduous and often droll practices of asceticism, and it is largely with these that their memory is associated. Yet the author of the ancient *Historia Monachorum* tells us that 'their chief concern is the love which they show to one another and towards such as by chance reach that spot', and again:

> But of their humility, their courtesy, their loving kindness, what am I to say when each man of them would have brought us into their own cell, not only to fulfil the due of hospitality, but still more . . . from gentleness and its kindred qualities which are learned among them with diverse grace but one and the same doctrine, *as if they had come apart from the world for this end.* Nowhere have I seen love so in flower, nowhere so quick in compassion, or hospitality so eager . . .[4]

There is importance in these quotations for the present renewal of religious life. For on the one hand immense efforts are being made to banish individualism, to make 'community' a deeply experienced and fulfilling reality. Words like 'sharing', 'dialogue', 'encounter' are repeated as if holy incantations. 'Togetherness' is imperative for some: meditating together, discussing together, working together, etc. – which is all very well if it is borne in mind that 'communion' is not quite the same thing as 'community', and that for some there will always be an inbuilt need for greater space between persons, for a solitude and privacy which is in no way a repugnance to love and genuine relatedness.

On the other hand, there is a fear among many religious that changes which in any way lessen the austerity of the life are eroding its very essence. They may not acknowledge it explicitly, but for them the monastic project is essentially a holy war waged against the world, the flesh and the devil, and they believe that tradition supports them. Indeed, it has often been held that community life is a mere concession to human weakness and that it developed as such from the earlier hermit life. This we have seen

94

not to be the case. Anyway, love, not austerity, was the gauge of perfection among the desert fathers. Rufinus Tyrannius visited the desert of Nitria about 371 and wrote of the recluses: 'They have indeed a great rivalry among them – it is who shall be more merciful than his brother, kinder, humbler, more patient.'

It would be difficult at any time to convey in the space of a few pages an adequate impression of the many differences between the orders in the manner of organizing and structuring their common life. A plethora of recent changes aggravates that difficulty excessively. Indeed, at present, there are often vast dissimilarities of life-style between the local communities of one order.

Almost every order or congregation has some kind of central authority which oversees and co-ordinates the life and work of all the houses, which are often in many different countries. In perhaps the majority of cases this central authority consists of a superior general and four or more counsellors. These are elected every six years by a general assembly or chapter made up of delegates representing the order as a whole. The delegates themselves are elected by the secret vote of everyone except novices, in such a way as to ensure proportional representation of each region in the order. As well as choosing a general council, this assembly has the right to legislate for the order as a whole, to modify existing legislation and determine general policies and principles. For example, a few years ago, the chapter of the Immaculate Heart of Mary Sisters in Los Angeles decided that their nuns should be allowed to undertake individually work other than the community's traditional teaching or hospital involvements. It determined that in their schools classes should never exceed thirty-five pupils, and that sisters not fully qualified in their professions were to be withdrawn for further studies. The chapter also decreed that the nuns could drop the title 'sister' if they wished, choose their own clothes and be given a small amount of pocket money. Each house, it declared, should choose its own forms and times of prayer and make adaptations that its own situation proved necessary. The Archbishop of Los Angeles opposed these decisions point by point, refusing to allow the nuns to work in his schools unless they returned to their former mode of life. The dispute became so complicated that 315 of the sisters, headed by the Mother General, decided to renounce their canonical status as religious, but to go on living as religious unofficially. Yet the chapter had every right to legislate as it did, and in recent years far more radical reforms have been made by such assemblies of other orders without any hierarchical interference.

There are congregations such as the Society of Jesus in which the superior general is elected for life, while the Order of St Benedict has an Abbot Primate chosen to hold office for twelve years by a congress bringing together every Benedictine abbot in the world.

The council – superior general and counsellors – does not have legislative powers. It meets regularly to survey the state of the order as a whole, examines reports sent in to it by each region and each house, and discusses particular problems and possibilities that may require its final decision. For example, a house may have decided that its work is no longer meeting local needs or that it cannot respond effectively to such needs. It may then request its own suppression and the redistribution of its members among other houses. To the council may pertain such powers as the appointment in each house of a local superior, although there are orders such as the Dominicans in which superiors at all levels are elected. Usually it is the council which pronounces finally upon the acceptance or rejection of candidates who wish to become novices or to be incorporated into the order by vow.

Regular visits are made by the superior general and counsellors to each of the houses, and various communication systems are devised such as permanent commissions for each aspect of the order's life and work, offering information, suggestions or objections to the council.

In the old, specifically monastic orders, like that of St Benedict, or in communities whose life is particularly ordered to contemplation, it is usual to find that each house is an autonomous unit. Its members do not move from one monastery to another. Superiors are elected and decisions such as the acceptance of candidates are made by the whole community.

As for life at the local level, perhaps it would be more interesting for readers if two existing communities, organized in very different ways, were described.

First visit the mother-house of an order, the Augustinian

Sisters of Meaux, which has been in existence since the thirteenth century. Although situated on the main road of a busy town on the outskirts of Paris, its high walls and immensely strong outer doors give it a fortress-like appearance as well as the assurance of a relatively secluded and tranquil environment. Of the forty nuns, about sixteen are now retired from professional work. The older and more infirm among them live separately in pleasant quarters with their own oratory and common-room from which they are able, by simply turning a switch, to listen to the lectures given downstairs, or to the liturgy in the main chapel. Two sisters, infirmarians, are particularly responsible for their care and comfort, while the other nuns, or their own relatives, are constant visitors. That the community has thought deeply about this stage of life is evidenced in their rule:

> Each of us will experience the process of ageing in an individual manner according to her personality and her past life. For most of us, however, in differing degrees, fear is intermingled with deepening joy, frustration with more assured peace, loneliness with richer communion. In one sense there is diminishment, in another increase. Our life is consummated in and through both . . . It is the responsibility of all of us to see that old age is an ever deeper experience of community and as productive as possible . . . Let there then be as little segregation as possible between the generations. This is deeply necessary, both to decrease loneliness and to foster mutual enrichment.

Several of the active sisters are employed in a work thought to be considerably needed in France – the care of old people, not in an impersonal 'home', but in four separate houses of single rooms. The buildings are within the convent grounds and the sisters are encouraged by their rule to 'regard these men and women as our own family, for so they are in Christ'. This work brings a small income to the community, as does the district nursing and parish work of four other sisters. It has to be subsidized, however, by contributions from every other house of the order, which are economically self-supporting.

Cooking, laundering, general administration, accountancy, cleaning and so on, are all done by the nuns with the help of a few 'au pair' girls. The sisters are dressed identically and their habits are made and repaired by two of them. Such necessities as stamps, note-paper and toilet articles are kept in a common store to be distributed as requested, and whenever a sister needs money she asks for it from the bursar on each separate occasion, and must subsequently hand in the account of its expenditure.

Care is taken that everyone has the professional training and re-training required for her work, the possibility of pursuing a particular talent – musical and artistic, for example – and access to sources of a wider culture. The younger nuns go regularly to Paris for courses of theological studies, and a lecture is given to all, once a week, by different priests. From time to time there are discussions in small groups of subjects about the religious ideal and its realization.

Four times a day the sisters come together in the church for liturgical prayer, the first at 6.15 a.m. On the heavy benches they take their places according to a certain order of precedence – at the back those in authority, then senior nuns and downwards. The offices of lauds, midday prayer, vespers and compline are composed of psalms sung to gentle monotonous melodies, reflective silences and prayers of intercession for various needs in the church and the world. All is taken from an office book commonly used in Roman Catholic communities. Whatever the inner and spiritual sentiments of those participating, either in the office or the daily Mass, the measure of aesthetic enjoyment and bodily awareness of each other seems to an observer very slight indeed.

Each sister is expected to set aside some time for meditative reading of the scriptures and not less than an hour a day for contemplative prayer. Arrangements are made so that a minimum of one day a month and five consecutive days a year are spent by each one in complete silence with leisure for reflection and prayer.

Meals in the long white refectory are almost as formal as the liturgy. Only during supper is conversation permitted, while breakfast and lunch are taken listening to music or to the reading of an article or book. Guests, unless religious themselves, normally eat in a separate dining-room – as much for their own convenience as for the privacy of the sisters.

The nuns do have some free time to themselves, but are expected to be present at the common recreation after lunch. Here they sit in a large circle, and if the art of conversation is not developed, that of the amusing narration is, at least by the extroverts.

Normally there will be about eight hours of work daily except on Sunday. The rule stipulates that each sister is to be assured of an annual holiday, its place and length of time to be worked out according to possibilities by the mutual consultation of sisters and superior.

The superior is appointed to hold office for not less than three and not more than six consecutive years. She has two assistants, one chosen by herself and the other elected by the community, and this triumvirate takes most of the decisions relative to the group as a whole.

An enormous amount is expected of the superior. She supervises all the administration in the house, co-ordinates its activities, is hostess for most of the visitors and tries always to be available to the sisters who so often wish to discuss with her their problems or aspirations, whether spiritual, psychological, domestic or professional. Above all she is expected to be a spiritual guide for each one and to stimulate the whole community to realize its ideals of prayer, fraternal communion and apostolic service. Where there is conflict, she is usually the arbitrator and, because trusted as a friend and helper by each, must avoid the appearance of partiality to any sister in particular.

Given differences of work, this is a fairly representative pattern of one mode of organizing the common life among both men and women religious. Slight modifications may have been made in many communities – conversation during meals, greater openness to outsiders, more imaginative variety in the liturgy, assurances of consultation in decision-making by those in authority, more contemporary forms of recreation and so on.

Another pattern which has been emerging over the last ten years is that of the small, informal community. It is rather the norm than the exception in Holland, is fast becoming so in America and Canada, and is not uncommon elsewhere, particularly in England and France. An example is one house of a Roman Catholic congregation which originated in Belgium about 200 years ago. Ten of its sisters live together in a large tenement house, one of a long row of dingy-looking buildings in a seedy corner of London. Within, it seems rather cluttered, for a number of randomly placed bookcases and shelves must substitute for a library. Some skilful modifications have made it possible for each sister to have a small room to herself, but, in contrast to the austere and impersonal 'cells' of the French convent, these are very evidently marked by the personality and interests of their occupiers. On the first floor a room has been made into a chapel, mercifully devoid of the benches which so impede movement and confrontation during the liturgy. Situated downstairs are a spacious kitchen, a tiny parlour and a long many-purpose room, cheerfully inelegant, with a dining table at one end and an assortment of armchairs and coffee tables at the other.

The nuns do not wear a religious costume and call each other by their Christian names rather than the usual 'Sister'. They share the housework and have a rota system for cooking the evening meal and keeping the house accounts. Some of them are students – in theology, psychology, child welfare. The others are employed for the most part within State organizations in nursing, teaching, counselling, occupational therapy, social welfare, religious education. All the incomes are pooled. Part of the total is put aside for the general house expenses such as food and rent, part for any needy individuals or groups; a proportion is sent to the mother house and each sister is given £10 a month. This must cover all her personal expenses – clothes, fares, stamps, stationery, toilet articles, two weeks annual holiday and the cost of a yearly retreat which is to be made in the convent or monastery of each sister's choice.

Here there is no superior; there are no 'seniors' and 'juniors', but one sister is nominated as the co-ordinator of the group and its official representative to the rest of the congregation. She, for example, keeps open the lines of communication between this and the other houses of the congregation, and particularly with its central authority. From time to time she would be required to evaluate the particular spiritual and apostolic strength and weaknesses of the community. Decisions are based upon the consensus reached during the weekly community meetings – lively affairs at which anything, material or spiritual, personal or communal, may be discussed and which are chaired by each sister in turn. If there is a deadlock, the group's co-ordinator may take an immediate decision.

The religious nature of the community is very explicit in these meetings. Everything discussed is evaluated in the terms of the

gospel and of the ideal of living a particular form of total dedication to God. It is clear that each one desires to grow in *all* the
dimensions of this ideal – the contemplative as well as the fraternal
and apostolic. A discussion of prayer is not an intellectual debate
so much as a sharing of joys and difficulties, aspirations and
obstacles. These sisters, in fact, spend as much, if not more, time
in silent contemplation and in meditating alone or together as do
those in the French mother house. Their liturgy is creative and
enjoyable. Lauds before breakfast and vespers after supper are
sometimes held in the chapel, sometimes in the sitting-room;
they are rarely taken from an office book but devised by one or a
few sisters. The eucharist is celebrated just before the evening
meal and varies in mood and manner – solemn or gay, quietly
meditative or full of music and movement.

Needless to say, there are no set 'recreations'. Each sister spends
her leisure-time according to her choice and possibilities, but
there are pleasant hours passed together around the supper table
or listening to music in the evening, or celebrating a special
occasion. Visitors, both men and women, are frequent, and
because they simply share, if they wish, meals, prayer and relaxa-
tion with the sisters, their presence seems less of a distraction
from the common life and duties than in the traditional convent,
where hospitality is more formal.

Now if, after having lived in both these communities, one were
to make a comparison in terms of what St Paul called the 'fruits
of the Spirit', i.e. love, joy, peace, patience, kindness, goodness,
trustfulness, gentleness and self-control, then one might ignore
the obvious differences and admit to being equally impressed in
both groups. For it is obvious that there is a remarkable spiritual
fervour in both houses in the sense that the majority, at least, of
their members are sincerely and enthusiastically striving to be
praying persons, giving, especially *for*giving persons.

The collective naïveté in so many communities, however, lies
precisely in ignoring the need to analyse and evaluate themselves
in other terms than those of a private morality, of inward and
individual virtue. They are aware of themselves as being involved
in a spiritual drama, which they are convinced is played out in
the heart, the inner centre of the self or perhaps of many 'selves'.
It is here that they endeavour to transform the Beast into Beauty,

101

the slave into a freeman, the hoarder of life into a gratuitous giver. They are hurt and bewildered at being described as 'inmates of a total institution' when they aim to be loving participants in a community of life. They dismiss as profound ignorance the accusation that they are hidebound in conventions and benighted in separation, when inner freedom and wisdom are all their striving. It is claimed that the outward conventions matter little, since only the heart's disposition is of decisive importance. Thus, it is not calling your companions 'Sister' or 'Mary', 'Brother' or 'John' that is of consequence, but loving and caring for them. What does it matter if you wear a religious costume or secular dress, since you should be concerned not with outer appearances but with the quality of your spirit? Neither democracy or oligarchy in themselves promote or lessen virtue and delicacy of conscience, so why favour one system rather than the other? And so it goes on. Yet such indifference is belied by the very resistance to change of structures, organization and style.

What such resistance reveals is in fact something that is perceived by the 'new' communities as of vital importance – the problem of language. Language, that is, in the widest meaning – the relation between our private and public world, between our inner integrity and the rules and forms of our society. Dress is language, so are our models of social intercourse, our patterns of authority and worship, the way we accord privilege or precedence and distribute responsibility. Our language not only expresses our inner self, but helps to shape its development. Where two or three are gathered together there is not only the possibility of meaningful one-to-one relationships in which each individual is responsible for his emotions, intelligence and spiritual aspirations. There are also conventions, and there is an organization relative to the corporate life of the group. A study of nineteenth-century manners would show that we divorce these two levels at our peril.

It is not suggested that the only alternatives of common life are the two patterns sketched above. For there are, in fact, other very attractive ways, such as that of Taizé, which so skilfully harmonizes the old and the new, contemplation and action, the intimacy of small groups and the space and privacy afforded by large monasteries. Nor is it ignored that there are communities which expressly aim at providing a semi-eremitical life, or at least a real possibility of physical solitude, and will organize themselves accordingly. Yet even here the members do come together at times, and should consider whether or not that 'membership of one another' which they appreciate mystically has authentic forms of expression.

It *is* suggested, though, that there is an inner contradiction in communities like the French mother house whose rule contains passages such as the following: 'The basic attitude of our fraternal life is the conviction of our positive responsibility for and deep need of each other . . . Let us, then, live turned towards each other, present to each other . . .' Is such an attitude adequately expressed and fostered by a liturgy in which individuals stand parallel to each other in hierarchical order, by meals in which the attention is directed towards a reading, by recreations in which the majority simply constitute an audience?

Moreover, where the superior has the dominant and multifaceted role which has been described, mutual need and responsibility tends to be associated predominately with the one exercising this office. He or she is expected as is none other to listen to the joys and sorrows, the hopes and difficulties of each member, and to offer as none other, support, encouragement, correction, counsel.

As for sharing responsibility in such communities, it has little chance of meaning more, in practice, than good-willed cooperation and the faithful execution of decisions made by superiors. No one is denying that these latter can be immensely kind and discerning, and take great pains to consult all concerned. Nor is it denied that refinement of conscience is expected of all. Nevertheless, the system itself is a manager/managed one or follows the pattern of command and obedience to be found in a family. This may have been no obstacle to fraternity in a feudal society which was hierarchical throughout, but today such an organization is inappropriate and inadequate, to say the least. We are educated for democracy. We need, therefore, guaranteed structures in which everyone participates as an equal and is expected to join in creating the forms in which a community expresses its life and responds to particular problems or possibilities.

Indeed at the local level, where the group is 'at home', there is

103

no absolute necessity for authority and responsibility to be represented by one or two persons. Surely authority lies ultimately in the community's ideals, and responsibility in the group consensus and in each individual's conscience? It is true that there are problems in having no officially appointed leader, as the small London community described above came to realize. At first a *laissez-faire* ethos prevailed, but only because the members had been accustomed to receive spiritual stimulus and practical organization mainly from *one* person. It gradually became able to provide both through other means – particularly the weekly community meetings. Members also became aware of the problem of unofficial 'natural' leaders who were often, with the best of intentions, dominative and manipulating. With a little time, however, and a growing understanding of group dynamics, the community learned how to counteract the oppressiveness of such persons while utilizing their insights and energy.

Where the community works together as a team, there may well have to be a formalized role-structure. More than sweetly chaotic good will and spontaneity is required to run a hospital or parish. But, unless religious are going to define themselves totally by their professional commitments, this functional pattern of relationships has no place among them outside the work-situation.

Perhaps for most people looking in on religious life the affective dimensions of relationships is of greater interest than the problem of social structures. Given that some form of enclosure system has been in force during the last few hundred years, it is not surprising that the most unreal images have been projected – absurdly romantic or stupidly cynical. As far as the heart is concerned, monasticism guarantees neither a perpetual unclouded summer's day nor a long winter of discontent.

There is, in a sense, a marvellous conspiracy in a convent or monastery – a conspiracy of belief and hope that makes love possible in fairly improbable circumstances. The very fact that you share so much of your life with the other members of the community, with few escape hatches, means that you are intensely aware of how foreign you may be from them – in nationality, education, past experience, intelligence and, above all, in taste. But normally, if you come to religious life and remain there, you

104

do so in virtue of an approach to reality that is called faith. You are certain of that which may not be visible – your own and other people's transcendence as made in the image of God. You do not look at others nor at the prospect of living together without some degree of beauty in your eyes, something analogous to inspiration in your mind. Michael Polanyi suggests that scientific discoveries are the fruit of what he calls 'anticipation' or 'creative desire'. And Saint-Exupery's 'Little Prince' says that what he likes about the desert is that somewhere it contains a well. Here is the kind of disposition that is meant by faith, and it moves a religious to discover, or set about discovering, the hidden riches in others, particularly those nearest others, the members of the community.

You, in turn, are sure in the name of all that brings you together, that it is with this in mind that you are regarded by others. Nothing is more releasing of all that is best in the personality than this mutual trust which precedes natural acceptability or lack of it. It does not blur differences, or lessen the pain of discordance, but it provides a kind of meeting-place where revelation and reconciliation become possible.

Prayer and worship are not quiet hiding-places from each other. They are rather the daily sources of a renewal of vision and courage in the creating of bonds which, here as elsewhere, may snap under the stress of friction and misunderstanding. No matter how the eucharist is celebrated, it is essentially a vivid word of God that tells us there is no communion of heart with him if that heart is deliberately closed to our 'other selves'. 'Although we are many, yet we are one bread, one body. Be what you see and receive what you are,' commented St Augustine. It is blasphemous to celebrate the sacrament of reconciliation and communion if it is not to be a reality in daily life.

The object of mediating upon the scriptures, or of silent contemplation, is not primarily to acquire biblical information or self-discipline. There is an Arab proverb which says: 'Come to me with your heart and I will give you my eyes.' And meditation or contemplation is this coming to God with the heart without projecting on to him our own vision and desires – but to receive his eyes, his 'infinitely gentle, infinitely suffering' understanding.

It is hardly necessary to say that in any religious community there will be tensions, unaccountable or accountable antipathies, clashes, irritations, a measure of anxiety, envy and outbursts of anger. They are certainly not tolerated with complacency, but they are not held to invalidate the project of communion nor to imply hypocrisy. What *is* held to be unacceptable is the drying-up of desire, the refusal to take any steps towards resurrecting concord, warmth, unity of heart and mind from the ashes of a particular failure. Almost any Rule has a passage like the following, which is a tissue of quotations from St Paul:

> Let us also bear one another's burdens, clothed in sincere compassion, in kindness and humility, gentleness and patience. Let us forgive one another as readily as God has forgiven us in Christ, never have grudges against others or allow any forms of spitefulness. So the body grows and is renewed in love day by day. Let us be true friends and sisters to one another in a warm, human and deeply personal manner . . . Let us combat selfishness, hardness of heart, possessiveness, striving to offer each other a trusting love, an effective care, loyalty, respect, responsibility. And let there never be jealousy or envy among us. For we are a community of unique persons and love, while making us one, calls each by name.[5]

Words, words, words? Perhaps, but do not underestimate the power of words and ideas in a society which refuses to live by bread alone.

In this matter of failure in loving relationships, religious have more help perhaps than many. Counselling, spiritual direction, the time for reflection are built into the life. In many communities there is not only the custom of one-to-one counselling, but a regular 'review of life' as it is called, in small groups. You may never have read a word of Freud or Jung, but you will have read, as a religious, Christ's parable of the weeds that are sown among the wheat, and St Paul's dramatic avowal that he found another law within himself grappling with his will for the good. You know that you cannot suppress these other forces by sheer will-power or wave a transforming wand over all that is wild and dark and instinctive within. But in coming to know, explore, accept as part of the self the jungle of instincts such as those for security, domination, destruction, submission, they may slowly become the very dynamism that transforms mere knowledge of the good into spontaneity, creativeness, courage and contemplation. You can sometimes be paralysed, prevented from doing anything because

106

you fear the evil within is so intermingled with the good that you are incapable of any really pure action. Yet in the parable the weeds were not uprooted from the field – they were burnt at the harvest. The harvest is every day, every moment that we try to give ourselves, and weeds will surely be burnt up in the forgiveness and understanding of the other.

Obviously, in any given community there will be more than social differences among the members. Every individual also has a particular temperament and character, a personality with its own history, wounds, prejudices, qualities and strengths. It is impossible, therefore, to make many generalizations as to the manner in which religious relate and express themselves on the psychological level. There are persons who constantly display their emotions. There are others who use disguises – who become the community clown, for example, or the detached, witty observer, or who tend to subsume their relationships under the concept of duty. Some are peculiarly gifted – their presence is all warmth, tenderness and availability. Others have been so hurt in their past life that, in spite of good will, trust and openness are as feared as they are desired. And just as some members require, on account of work or illness, an extra measure of the community's material goods, so these persons have to be given extra marks of affection, care and inner support.

One could continue at great length. The point is that love within a religious community – which should extend outwards – is not a vague moral disposition, nor a purely verbal ideal. It is a human affair experienced at many levels, fraught with difficulty and delight.

At times the very delight evokes its own difficulties. Just as lovers may find it difficult not to feel threatened, but possibly enriched in their intimacy by acknowledging their separateness, so a celibate needs time and experience to integrate concrete experiences of love and communion into his fundamentally solitary way. It is extremely unlikely that a person will go through religious life without feeling for one or more persons, within or without the community, of one sex or the other, emotions of the strongest and tenderest love. Emotions, that is, which focus all a person's awareness, expectancy, generosity and sensitivity upon another who will therefore preoccupy the heart for at least the

107

early stages of the relationship. And it is almost as unlikely that this will occur without the subject supposing that the ground has gone from under his commitment to God and to others in celibate love.

The ground may only have gone, of course, from under an all-too-shallow existence. The religious may be more preoccupied with the preoccupation than with the other person, and if so, risks ignoring the presence of God in this particular burning bush. It can be difficult, however, unless one is already spiritually and affectively very mature to receive gratefully and respond warmly to such a love while at the same time not being able to offer the other an exclusiveness of concern nor its expression in sexual intimacy. One may find this impossible and destructive, and discover thereby that one has never really chosen religious life for what it is. Or again, there are persons whose affectivity has been only minimally involved in relation to God. Neither on coming to the convent/monastery nor subsequently has there been a touch of fire or holy madness in the heart, but rather a mixture of philanthropy and religiosity. For these, too, a deep human love may point away from religious life. Indeed, it is far better for them to search for the possibility of wholeness elsewhere than to remain stunted or stoical within sexual solitude.

For the majority, however, these experiences are understood – by some intuitively, by others with help and counsel – as included within their growth in celibate love. They reveal so much about oneself, others and God – and God is not, in these events, an observer but the prime mover. It takes a little time before the somewhat shattering effects of the explosion settle down and the precious gold, the now more available resources in the heart can enrich prayer, fraternal life and professional work. It becomes easier to live in a genuinely heartfelt manner the entirely unpossessive love that is both the pain and the joy of the celibate. And it becomes clearer that there are no substitutes for fully sexual love. The way of religious life with its passion for God and for loving others in God may be equally fulfilling for those called to it, but it *is* an alternative way, excluding significant possibilities. It is well to be very clear about these exclusions, since it is not unknown for religious, through being naïve or dishonest, to arouse expectations in others that they are not going to meet.

It must be added, finally, that the whole question of being integrally chaste in religious life is seen far too dramatically from outside. If it were a perpetual battle, there assuredly would be no vocation, for the call is not just to give up, but to give. Becoming a religious is not a cold choice of the will, but a response to God who is attracting the whole being – the affectivity as well as the intellect. Yet there will undoubtedly be suffering. The absence of one enclosing other in your life is a loneliness that no amount of fraternal or apostolic love can overcome. But then, you do not want it to be overcome if that is your place to be.

## NOTES

1. Martin Buber, *Between Man and Man*, Fontana Books 1961, p. 38.
2. Ibid., p. 39.
3. *The Rule of Taizé*, Les Presses de Taizé 1967 (in French and English), pp. 135–9.
4. Rufinus, *Historia Monachorum*, ch. 21.
5. Rule of Life, Augustinian Sisters, London.

# 6    Prayer and Action

Degrees of paranoia affect many religious who move in secular circles. Refusing to wear a monastic costume, in public at least, has been one attempt to counter its cause. So often wearing the black cloth has the effect of waving a red rag! Even among relatives, friends or colleagues, religious are constantly battered by questions that are heavy with prejudice, which is understandable enough if one displays private choices in public by symbolic dress or ornament.

Religious are associated with prayer and 'good works'. Both are suspected – prayer and withdrawal for what we get out of them, work and involvement for what we put in. Prayer is thought to be a wasteful expenditure of time and energy on an activity which has no 'useful' end-product; work, even when it is completely secular, is suspected of being a means to infiltrate society at its most vulnerable in order to inject a dose of religion.

The history of religious life is not such that we can make a response of injured innocence. So much of our literature on prayer is complicated and pretentious, and evaluation of work in terms of 'conversions' is, to say the least, not unknown. Yet at the same time a plea must be made once again to both interrogated and interrogators for awareness of the problem of language.

Religious often forget that words such as 'meditation' and 'contemplation' are used in so many different ways that it cannot be presumed that they convey what may be intended. Do they refer to techniques or to a total way of life? Do they apply to specifically religious reflections and sentiments or can they include philosophical speculation, 'mind-blowing ecstasy', a certain receptive attitude towards reality? And how technical words such as 'liturgy' or 'apostolate' sound! Moreover, they evoke images and ideas which relative to the listener's experience might have been totally negative. Thus for many, 'liturgy' speaks only of barren, joyless and unintelligible Sunday services. Or if 'apostolic zeal' means anything, it is probably associated with the memory of persuasion – to accept dogmas, to reverse morality, to 'practise' religion sacramentally.

On the other hand, some sympathy is called for. A dancer is not always the best person to verbalize the experience and meaning of the dance – for the primary language is in the movement itself. Similarly, it may be hateful for a praying person to conceptualize the experience of prayer. The language is in the experience itself, the 'happening' between the contemplator and the contemplated, the yielding of a fragment of significance, meaning, value, from the reality – a word, an event, the increased 'aliveness' in understanding and love, in pain and joy. Such language is shared, not primarily in words, but in the life-enkindling quality of the contemplative's existence. Indeed this sharing which is life-enkindling is the ultimate meaning of the term 'apostolate' as used in religious life, where it may refer to anything from preaching a sermon to lecturing on economics, from cooking meals to research in paleontology. It may even refer simply to living religious life in so far as this radiates and helps in any way at all to inspire and deepen another's existence. Some lines from a poem of D. H. Lawrence put it well:

And if, as we work, we can transmit life into our work,
life, still more life rushes into us to compensate, to be ready
and we ripple with life through the days . . .

Give and it shall be given unto you
is still the truth about life.
But giving life is not so easy . . .
It means kindling the life-quality where it was not,
even if it's only in the whiteness of a washed pocket-handkerchief.[1]

Prayer and action. It may be necessary to distinguish between them mentally, and even, as in religious life, to make corresponding divisions of time. Yet they are two movements that belong to one another and flow in and out of one another. They should more and more be simultaneous in time – not simply in virtue of a good intention but in the way we approach and experience our activity. The ultimate aim is not to pray prayers, but to pray our life, and

111

the more receptive a person is, the more he or she is likely to be creative, a transmitter of life.

These considerations may indicate a first answer to the two suspicions that prayer is a waste of time and that in their activity religious are involved in a bid for power. Time is only *wasted* by contemplation or celebration in the view of neurotically hyperactive persons, or of a market-orientated society. There is no other product of prayer than a self which according to its own measure and rhythm becomes progressively wiser, more imaginative and courageous in its responses to reality.

Secondly, whatever happens in practice, in principle activity is prostituted if it is a means of pressurizing others or imposing upon them our moral and religious options. It is ironical indeed that the church so often condemns fascism and totalitarianism on these grounds when many of its members – including monks and nuns – use the same methods. Human beings are naturally arrogant enough to be generous, to generate the life-quality where it is not. In religious life this may take many forms besides washing pocket handkerchiefs – alleviating the impoverishment of sickness, ignorance, loneliness, old age, responding to the need for truth, for a saving word, for indications of transcendence. In all cases it is worthless, as St Paul reminds us, unless it is an activity of love. Basically, all needs are a need to *be* which is certainly not met by a manipulative and dominating imposition of self. But our aggressive wills can only be modified and complemented by developing the contemplative pole of our being. When whatever activity is indicated by the word 'apostolate' is degraded into a crusade, there is a divorce between prayer and action. When enthusiasm is split from a reverence for being, there something is vastly wrong, not with enthusiasm itself, but with its source in the heart. The fear of the Lord, which is equivalent to a reverence for being, is the beginning of wisdom.

So far we have been deliberately vague in the use of terms in order to suggest that life in the monastery or convent, as elsewhere, has to be an organic whole. Prayer is trivialized if it is not lived in relation to the high or humble events, the relationships, the objects, the work and leisure that make up our existence. But in religious life prayer is not only a quality of our existence, it is also a specific activity with several forms: reflection, meditation, contemplation and the various kinds of celebration that are called liturgy. The assumption is that we shall hardly live as contemplative and worshipful persons *all* the time unless *some* time is poetically wasted in those periods of stillness or celebration in which we try to find and express the significance of our life. Moreover, it is assumed that such meditative withdrawal and ritual festivity are human needs as basic as those for food, sleep, work, love. The contemporary rebirth in society of mysticism and the festive spirit may be the re-emergence of such needs, suppressed by the cumulative effect of industrialization, technocracy and a crude notion of 'factuality'.

Before attempting to describe some of the ways in which religious practise the various ways of prayer, it is perhaps well to remind readers that similar forms of this activity are found in most people's lives, even if they acknowledge no supernatural order. The rhythm that religious impose upon their existence in a more or less formal way – a time to give and a time to waste, a time to participate and a time to contemplate, a time to work and a time to celebrate – is quite informally adopted elsewhere – and without any religious reference. Most people know what it is to be still enough for some reality – a person, a busy street or peaceful valley, music, a word, an event – to speak to them, to reveal both itself and something more than itself. At such times a person can be said to meditate or contemplate. Experiences akin to mysticism are not unknown to most of us:

> . . . the unattended
> Moment, the moment in and out of time,
> The distraction fit, lost in a shaft of sunlight,
> The wild thyme unseen, or the winter lightning,
> Or the waterfall, or music heard so deeply
> That it is not heard at all, but you are the music
> While the music lasts.[2]

As for liturgy, its secular equivalents are dance, drama, pageants, carnivals, pop festivals, the immense variety of ways in which society or individuals creatively embody fantasy, relive their past, anticipate their future, celebrate the ancient mysteries of love, suffering and death. In fact we know what liturgy is about every time we hold a party and with its symbolism transform the opaque and repetitious nature of 'everyday' into a space where meaning, wonder and blessing might occur.

Whoever accepts existence, love, friendship, food, care, as a gift knows what the prayer of thanksgiving means. Whoever refuses to curse the world for its pain and its death but rather stretches himself to the measure of an impossible hope, knows what it means to pray that ultimately we shall be delivered from all evil. And those desires, in the night of human longing, for the world to be a place of justice, love, mercy and peace, are they not equivalent to the prayer: 'Thy kingdom come . . . on earth as it is in heaven'?

The convent or monastery is consciously intended to be a school of prayer and a community of worship. Moreover, in Christian monasticism, as distinct from the way of Buddha or various forms of secular mysticism, there is an explicitly God-ward perspective and a Christ-centred reference. Diverse measures are taken to provide a milieu favourable to contemplative living and opportunities to step aside from work in order to meditate or celebrate life together in God. A rather misleading distinction is made between 'contemplative' and 'active' communities. It really refers to the institution rather than the individual. A contemplative institute is something of a research centre in the art of prayer, and like most research centres is more or less withdrawn from society to pursue its specialist ends. No directly apostolic work is undertaken – at least not by the institute as such. But work – apart from the work that is prayer – there is indeed. Not only are there multiple domestic and administrative tasks, but exigencies of study, of developing individual talents and earning a living. Contemplatives may have large farms; produce perfume, as the Cistercians, and hand lotions, as the Trappists at Caldey; tonic wine, as the monks of Buckfast Abbey; liqueurs, as at the Grande Chartreuse; pottery, as at Prinknash. They may have printing presses or make altar breads and liturgical vestments, or keep a guest house, and so on. Today, however, there is a movement among contemplatives to re-situate and reorganize themselves. Needless to say, it is frowned upon by the Vatican, which favours, particularly for women, a strict enclosure system and physical separation from society. Some are moving into the city, living in an ordinary house or apartment, taking up part-time

114

work in a factory, an office, a social-welfare organization. Or they are developing along the lines of the Abbey of Boquen, described in Chapter 3, where outsiders come and go at will, where all are welcome to share the experiences of the monks, their joys and sorrows, their search for truth. In these changes the value of a life specializing in contemplation and worship is not questioned. Dom Bernard of Boquen defined his position thus:

> I should like to say clearly that I have the highest regard for the values of monasticism which, without being specifically Christian, can be lived according to the gospel, and, far from minimizing their importance, I believe that our century is especially in need of them. Far from despising or destroying these values, then, I believe that they merely need to be reformulated in a modern way, free from all legalism, formalism or phariseeism.

In 1969 Sister Margaret Rowe left her Carmel in Wales to found an experimental contemplative community in Canada. She describes her group of sisters in this way:

> They are contemplative in spirit, yet not separated from the rest of the community, but integrated into the life of the parish. They attend the parish church for Mass, and although they have a small oratory . . . in their home, they do not have a private chapel or traditional choir, but are experimenting with various biblical services, psalms and scripture readings to replace the unvarying monastic office. They are not supported by parish or diocese, but work to provide their maintenance at part-time jobs which are not inimical to the contemplative orientation and which allow time for prayer life and for some form of charitable but gratuitous service to those among whom they live. The Sisters . . . are not social workers, since that is not their vocation, nor do they have the necessary training. But . . . they hope to be able to perform voluntary work in that vast no-man's-land which neither the welfare services nor the official church apostolate reaches: the lonely, the alienated, those hungry for some understanding and experience of prayer, but who have nowhere to go for discussions, advice, or merely a place where they are assured of an atmosphere of quiet for reflection, and for contact with and sharing between those who have dedicated their lives to prayer while remaining in touch with the world and its needs.[3]

There will always be some, however, who wish for more complete solitude and withdrawal from society. Whether they live alone or in communities, they should not be charged *a priori* with selfishness and uselessness. The very least that can be said in their

115

favour is that they do not contribute to three contemporary problems: over-population, unemployment and ecological pollution! They should – and nowadays do – earn their own frugal living, and with an economy in society that may not be one of abundance, but is not one of scarcity, why insist that everyone should be, in one way or another, on the assembly line? The usual ecclesiastical defence of contemplatives of this sort is insistence upon their value as a source of grace for society through their prayer and example. But this is really only trying to answer philistine objectors in their own pragmatic terms – in terms of production and usefulness. We know very little about how prayer affects persons other than those praying, and as for the value of witness, these solitaries make every effort to escape the public eye. No, the primary value of such a life is that it meets the deep needs of those who embrace it. Its use is not in the production of goods but in helping the development of good persons. If a married couple have no children, shall we dismiss their marriage as 'sterile' and 'useless'? Does one ever marry simply to procreate? Similarly, if some degree of wisdom and loving-kindness, some glimpse, too, of God, 'as through a glass darkly', if these and not apostolic works are the only fruits of a life 'hidden with Christ in God', is there not some purpose to this waste? It may be objected that to live in such confinement and relative isolation is to preclude the possibility of psychic growth. Certainly it is true that most of the important limitations that we impose upon ourselves by our commitments for the sake of love, or art, or our career, or faith, exclude the development of potentialities that might have flowered had we made other choices. But it is a fallacy to think that the quality of our living is necessarily enhanced by the extent of our experience. Jane Austen seemed to delight in the fact that the material from which she created her books was so limited: 'the little bit (two inches wide) of ivory on which I work'. She achieved her own unique brilliance within such confinement, and it would be absurd to complain that her art lacked qualities manifest in that of writers whose experience of life was vaster in extent. Like Jane Austen, though, the recluse has to like his or her limits and bring to the small bounded space enough intelligence and desire to dig deep. 'To him who *has* shall be given more.'

116

Contemplation is concerned with the depth rather than the extent of our experience. But it is only at a certain depth that one can say with the Eastern mystic: 'Without stirring abroad one can know the whole world.' Thomas Merton lived in the vast silence of a Trappist monastery and for a time as a hermit. He insisted that the solitary does not wish to affirm himself to be different, withdrawn, elevated, separate from the common herd.

On the contrary, he realises, though perhaps confusedly, that he has entered into a solitude that is really shared by everyone. It is not that he is solitary while everybody else is social, but that everyone is solitary . . . he remains united to others and lives in profound solidarity with them, but on a deeper and mystical level . . . He realises that he is one with them in the peril and anguish of their common solitude, not the solitude of the individual only but the radical and essential solitude of man . . . Hence his solitude is the foundation of a deep, pure and gentle sympathy with all other men . . . the emptiness is for the sake of the fullness, the awareness of the divine mercy transforming his own emptiness and turning it into the presence of perfect love.[4]

A reproach that could be made to contemplative orders in general is that their life is not contemplative *enough*. The organization in the monastery or convent is too tight, fragments the day with far too many summons to liturgical prayer, and thus promotes a kind of busyness that is inimical to the contemplative spirit. One is reminded of the horrid Eliza's advice to her lazy sister Georgiana in *Jane Eyre*: 'Take one day; share it into sections; to each section apportion its task: leave no stray unemployed quarters of an hour, ten minutes, five minutes – include all; do each piece of business with method, with rigid regularity. The day will close almost before you are aware that it has begun.'[5] Take warning – Charlotte Brontë disposes of Eliza by placing her in a nunnery, reflecting through Jane Eyre, 'The vocation will fit you to a hair, much good may it do you.'[6]

In all communities, whether enclosed or apostolic, silence and the possibility of periodic solitude are valued as precious aids to spiritual growth. Times and places are often imposed by rule, but at present the tendency is to allow the individual to choose his own forms and periods of quiet and withdrawal according to his own needs and rhythm of life and work. It is thought that too much emphasis has been placed upon external silence, whereas

117

what matters is the inner stillness, with all the loneliness, the fear of the dark, the sheer blankness that may be attendant upon it. We would fatally ignore our bodiliness if we thought that this inner silence could be achieved without any outer quiet. Nevertheless, imposing silence by law only leads to absurdities such as the antics of sign language which, until recently, was used by the Trappists for communication other than that which absolutely required conversation.

As for meditation, contemplation, liturgy in religious life, there is a great variety of ways in which these are understood and practised even within the one community. In general, meditation is a way of exploring reality in a manner that is at once relaxed and highly attentive. The aim of the various methods is to achieve an inner unity, a being 'put together' so that we may be gifted with perception and clarity. In this clarity one can hear and see, and if there is a difference between meditation and contemplation it is that the latter is the awaited yet unexpected hearing and seeing with one's whole unified being. What is the object of such awareness? It may be a text, a thought, the underlying unity of all things, God's personal presence, your own self, a relationship, a joy or a frustration, the place in which you sit, an event, a commonplace object. Anything may be seen as for the first time and with a joy-bearing significance. There is a story in the New Testament of Jesus healing a blind man. Mark delightfully recounts the stages: 'The man, who was beginning to see, replied, "I can see people; they look lie trees to me, but they are walking about." Then . . . he saw clearly; he was cured and he could see everything plainly and distinctly.' Meditation is this conscious endeavour to allow the doors of our perception to be opened that we may discover new depths, see new connections, be surprised with new insight. It is equally correct to call this the work of the Spirit of Christ or to explain it in terms of psychological process, for the power of God neither opposes nor runs parallel to man's power but rather makes it to be, is creative even of man's freedom. The fact that at each instant we receive our being and power from God does not therefore make them less real nor less our own. Like the cured man, religious would attribute their renewal of vision to Jesus – to his Spirit, the Spirit of Truth, which he said would guide men into all truth. Moreover the scriptures, and especially the New Testament, are used as precious sources for meditation. They are not studied at this time, but listened to with the heart. 'Come to me with your heart and I will give you my eyes.' The approach is meditative. It is an openness and receptivity by which we risk being changed by another, being illuminated by the other's understanding. It is for the sake of developing faith – of seeing the world as if with the eyes of God.

There are old and new methods used in religious life – one person may have several approaches to prayer. Yoga positions are being used ever more frequently to achieve the necessary relaxed attentiveness. Sometimes writing meditatively proves useful. This is not new. Augustine, Bernard, Catherine, Teresa, Pope John, Dag Hammarskjöld seem to have meditated in this way at times. One religious has said recently that writing a journal is for him 'a way into prayer, an openness to contemplation, a celebration and remembering, a discovery and a centering'. Or small groups are formed to meditate together with a time of silence and a time of sharing. Other groups are more ecstatic – each participant is silent until moved to express in the presence of God and of each other, the spirit's longings, joy or grief or ardent desire.

One of the difficulties about prayer is to find one's own style and, for the religious in particular, to unify life so that prayer is not one duty among others but a way of unfolding from obscurity what is already there in the reality which we are and in which we live. We should be free from compulsiveness – we do not need to pray for *God's* sake, but for our own. The Father, as Christ said, knows our needs – he does not have to be informed of them, but we may need to articulate them, to become aware of our situation, to express our faith and hope and love in words and gestures as useless and as beautiful as a gift of flowers.

Liturgy is social rather than private prayer. It is not an exercise in stillness and meditation, but is a community's festive expression of worship, dramatizing in song and ritual movement its faith and hope and thanksgiving. For several hundred years now there has been an enormous amount of liturgical prayer in religious life – daily celebration of the eucharist and anything from four to seven periods a day for the liturgy known as the office. This last has developed from the custom of the early Christian community of praying at the hours which marked the main

119

divisions of the day. The night office which some contemplatives observe developed from the nocturnal prayer vigils that were held on Easter Eve, and gradually extended to Sundays and other festivals. Each section of the office is made up of a number of psalms, canticles, a hymn, a scripture reading and some intercessory prayers.

The reasons for so much liturgy are summed up in the rule of one order:

> We pray in common not only to express in words the worship of our lives and our waiting on the Lord together, but as representatives of the whole church, desiring to be for all men, for all creation, a voice of praise and supplication: 'On your walls, Jerusalem, I set watchmen. Day and night they must never be silent ... who keep Yahweh mindful.'

That rule also stresses that both with regard to inner attitude and external expression these celebrations should be true prayer, evocative, beautiful and meaningful. All too frequently, however, the liturgy in religious houses is boring, dull and lifeless – its arteries are hardened, it lacks imagination; it has neither the solemn beauty of the ancient monastic ritual nor the liberating festivity of secular celebrations. It frequently has no artistic integrity and, saddest of all, many communities ignore the fact that liturgy *is* the *art* of celebrating and dramatizing our history of salvation.

Harvey Cox in his book *The Feast of Fools* writes: 'Ritual should lure people into festive fantasy, put them in touch with the deepest longings of the race, help them to step into the parade of history, and ignite their capacity for creation.'[7] All too often, if this happens during monastic liturgy, it is not in virtue of its artistic forms but because of the richness of mind and heart gained through life and contemplation which religious bring to their common worship, enabling them to strike some living water from the rock. Once again the liturgy is a language problem – its movement and music, its songs and ritual are a public language that must express the dreams and hopes that God himself inspires in us. It will necessarily be a dead language if the things that God has joined together: religion and life, spirit and matter, intellect and emotion, divine and human, are torn asunder. Moreover liturgy must change its forms if it is to express man's consciousness which alters with changes in his environment – cultural, social, economic and political changes. This is not to deny that we have an ever-old, ever-new message to hear and see in the words and gestures of the liturgy – liberation: our exodus from the captive ways of self and society; death and resurrection: the letting-go of fear and mean timidity of heart to respond with love and courage to the demands of life. But we must *be able* to hear and see, which demands that the medium shall correspond with the message.

So at the moment there are some few communities who have temporarily ceased to pray regularly in common in order to find themselves anew, and, from a renewed consciousness of their relationships to each other and to their world, seen within the all-embracing relationship with God through Christ, create more meaningful forms of worship.

In many other communities the sheer weight and number of liturgical periods has been reduced, most frequently to one period in the morning and one in the evening. This search for one's own group-identity and needs and rhythm is not at all a reaction against prayer itself. Rather it is a reaction against stagnation, an attempt to break out of a mediaeval pattern of life and a mediaeval understanding of worship. And there is so much love and intelligence and desire among religious that the admission of failure and inadequacy will surely be only a brief winter, harbouring in its seemingly barren earth a new season's growth.

Finally, a word about the various activities of religious in society. It has already been stated, but should be stressed, that the *raison d'être* of religious life is not to provide the church with special task-forces. One is neither more nor less of a religious in taking on some activity with and for the wider community, rather than remaining within the religious house in a life of intense contemplation and worship, involved in work that does not directly touch society. Religious are not persons whose vocation *as* religious is primarily to be a member of or an auxiliary to the clergy. If religious life as such does contribute to the varied beauty of the life of the church or the world, it is essentially by virtue of its particular life-form, the manner in which its members open themselves to the Spirit of God, their 'emptiness for the sake of fullness'. For some a ministry or service, a task of one kind or another within secular society, will be integral to their vocation, will be the way in which their solitude opens out to solidarity.

Most people know that many male religious become priests. Men or women are extensively involved in parish or mission work, catechetics or religious art, literature, music. For centuries religious have worked in education, medicine and various forms of social welfare. Recently in Europe and America, where the state or secular voluntary organizations are equipped to meet people's material or psychological needs, many religious are either working as individuals in and with these secular bodies, or moving into areas where help is more desperately required. In England such moves are relatively few and far between, nor is there here as much awareness as there should be among religious of the political implications of Christianity and of the need to change the structures of society so that they may reflect better the utopia that we call the kingdom of God. A short while ago a Cistercian abbot in Ireland, whose monastery had been searched by troops, told his television interviewers that he had no political comment to make as politics were no affair of men seeking God. On the other side of the Atlantic two other religious, the Berrigan brothers, were in gaol for having destroyed army draft cards. Four years previously nuns were stoned while taking part in Martin Luther King's freedom marches, stoned, as they themselves said, 'by the Christian kids we had told it was enough to go to Sunday Mass and eat Friday fish'! One marvellous sister has written a racy account of her swift political education. She went to live and work in a Chicago slum area. She found rat-infested boarding-houses, grossly overcrowded.

The original idea, I guess, was to teach these families how to live in the best possible way in their surroundings. But it took us close to thirteen minutes in the place to realise that these surroundings were not the sole responsibility of the 150 people who lived there. Somebody owned this place and was collecting 95 dollars a month from each one of these families for the dubious privilege of existing there. So we assumed our dumb-nun look and marched into the office of the biggest cigar-smoking slum landlord in Chicago. Of course . . . he would co-operate 102 per cent . . . Only we were even dumber than we thought. We were so dumb we didn't even realise that he needed a reputation saver and we were it. We were so extremely dumb we couldn't see that our services in the building were giving him an excuse to perpetuate a horror that should have been burned in a new Chicago fire.[8]

The awareness that the ills in society have to be healed in their root causes is having painful consequences in religious communities. In parts of France, Italy and Latin America, religious are beginning to realize that their institutions for the care of the old, of orphans or of the destitute, their schools and hospitals and relief work for the poor, are sustaining the complacency of the state and unwittingly helping to maintain gross injustices in their society. On the other hand, they fear to withdraw while needs are so widespread and political reform so uncertain.

Another problem in orders and congregations involved in traditional works such as teaching or nursing is that many now have schools and hospitals where the fees can only be met by the economically favoured. One of the reasons for this is that some communities sustain their non-remunerative works by the profits gained in their fee-paying institutes. Another is that in countries such as our own, where secular bodies provide education and health care, independent schools and hospitals have no means of surviving and of meeting required standards without charging fairly substantial fees. But within these communities the usefulness of such survival is vigorously questioned by many members. The argument has been that religious should be able to guarantee that Christian values pervade their work so that the atmosphere and policies of a school or hospital may be harmonized with the inspiration and ethical principles of the gospel. Now, however, many religious feel that such institutions run counter to the spirit of the gospel, at least indirectly. For there is the danger of their contributing to a ghetto-like mentality in Christians and of turning Christianity into an ideology or sub-culture within society. Secondly, rising costs now necessitate charging fees that only the fairly affluent can afford. How many mothers from the lower-paid working class could afford to have their babies in the private maternity homes run by sisters? How many such parents could send their children to the private schools owned by communities of monks, nuns or brothers? Happily there is an ever more acute realization that independence, if at all desirable for an institute,

123

is too costly in terms of that freedom to serve the under-privileged that is given to religious by their whole life-form.

It is not too well known by the general public that religious may be involved in almost any kind of work. There are psychologists, sociologists, scientists, miners, factory-workers, astronomers, librarians, cleaners, home-helps, poets and flight-nurses in aeroplane-hospitals, and at least one nun, Sister Lucy Faciana, is a mayor, of the town of St Leo in Central Florida! The very fact that it should occasion some surprise that persons dedicated in a particular way to God are involved in such secular tasks is evidence of the treacherous divorce that religious themselves have helped to bring about – the divorce between God and his world, the divorce between Jesus the person and Christ the Lord of history.

This is the house that God is building – not so much the church but the world, building it into a fully human community. There is a sense in which it is true to say that God himself, in and through our personal and cosmic history, is struggling to find expression. The world is the place of God's becoming; the Word of his wisdom is to be enfleshed in our humanity. In our stupidity and brutality it is God himself who is in agony, and being put to death 'all the day long', as St Augustine commented of Christ. And whenever we strive to do the things that make for peace, justice, liberation and love, there God's resurrection is finding expression. The poet Rilke asks us to live our life 'as a painful and beautiful day in the history of a great gestation' and tells us that . . . the least

> We can do is to make
> His becoming
> Not more difficult for Him
> Than the earth
> Makes it for the Spring
> When it wants to come.[9]

So, then, everything matters, and it is sufficient for a religious to find in a given work, whether as a labourer or an economist, a theologian or a district-nurse, the possibility of expressing hope and love, of humanizing the world and allowing God's life to break through it. The Jesuit, William Van Roo, in his book *The*

124

*Mystery*, indicates the approach that should be ours as Christians at work in the city of man:

> We do not compete with other particular problem-solvers, trying to reserve an area which is our sacred domain. We do not attempt to offer a specific Christian science or technology. We can hope to bring a Christian wisdom, a Christian understanding of man, a Christian love and sense of justice, to bear on all the problems of the city of man. We can hope to read in human history and in the achievements of man dimensions which revelation and faith alone disclose. These dimensions reveal a greater dignity and a nobler destiny and they inspire a stronger love and hope. We can hope that the vision of that dignity and destiny, and the experience of that love and hope, can fit us to co-operate with greater efficacy in solving the problems which are the concern of all men of good will.[10]

Whether in the city or marginal to it, whether involved in an active or contemplative manner in the affairs of society, religious are perhaps odd women, odd men out. Their task today is to shed the oddness that simply reflects a cultural backwardness and deepen the oddness of being men and women whose hearts are always poor and empty, hungry and thirsty because of their passion for God. In all but a handful of communities today, numbers are dwindling and there is only a thin stream of new members. Far from being a tragedy, this is a good. For it must force religious to look at their double foolishness – the one linked to a dynamic conservatism altogether opposed to their vocation, the other constitutive of that calling, the forging of a path to life through that particular wilderness into which God's spirit leads them. There are panicky voices in the church urging Christians to 'foster vocations', to pray and work that religious orders may once again have many 'recruits'. Such persons seem to understand nothing at all – their anxiety stems from identifying religious with their activities. They miss the sheer man- and woman-power that religious bring to the various works – ecclesiastical and secular – of the church, and want the security of knowing that a certain group of people in the Christian community is daily at prayer and striving for personal holiness. But neither good works, nor prayer, nor holiness, integral as they may be to religious life, are specific to it. Religious life is the fruit of a subjective experience of the love of God, effected by the Spirit who makes eunuchs of some 'for the sake of the kingdom of heaven'.

Of its very nature it is for the few, rather than the many – not because it is a superior way but because it is a strange and paradoxical one – a hair's breadth away from *un*holy madness. But if this life-form is invented *from* love, then, and only then, will it develop in and towards love. In the absurdity of sexual solitude one might then become slowly refined in heart through prayer, human communion, self-knowledge and service of others. Certainly God has no other purpose for any of us on earth than that we should become loving persons contributing each in our own way to putting together his broken body in the world.

## NOTES

1. D. H. Lawrence, 'We are Transmitters', *The Complete Poems of D. H. Lawrence*, Heinemann & the Viking Press, NY, p. 449. Used by permission of Laurence Pollinger Ltd, and the estate of the late Mrs Frieda Lawrence.

2. T. S. Eliot, 'The Dry Salvages', *Collected Poems*, Faber & Harcourt Brace Jovanovich, NY 1963, pp. 212 f.

3. Sister Margaret Rowe in *The Catholic Gazette*, December 1970, p. 12.

4. Thomas Merton, *Disputed Questions*, Hollis and Carter 1961 pp. 188, 189, 192.

5. Charlotte Brontë, *Jane Eyre*, ch. 21.

6. Ibid., ch. 22.

7. Harvey Cox, *The Feast of Fools*, Harvard University Press 1969, p. 81.

8. Sister Matthias Rinderer OSF, *The New Nuns*, Sheed and Ward 1968, p. 110.

9. Rainer Maria Rilke. I am unable to locate the poem from which the lines are taken.

10. W. A. Van Roo SJ, *The Mystery*, Gregorian University Press, Rome 1971, pp. 360 f.